LOGIC GAMES

FOR
WANNABE LAWYERS

MARK ZEGARELLI

PUZZLE
WRIGHT
PRESS

New York

**PUZZLE
WRIGHT
PRESS**

New York

An Imprint of Sterling Publishing
1166 Avenue of the Americas
New York, NY 10036

ISBN 978-1-4549-1202-6

Distributed in Canada by Sterling Publishing
⅝ Canadian Manda Group, 664 Annette Street
Toronto, Ontario, Canada M6S 2C8
Distributed in the United Kingdom by GMC Distribution Services
Castle Place, 166 High Street, Lewes, East Sussex, England BN7 1XU
Distributed in Australia by Capricorn Link (Australia) Pty. Ltd.
P.O. Box 704, Windsor, NSW 2756, Australia

For information about custom editions, special sales, and premium and
corporate purchases, please contact Sterling Special Sales at 800-805-5489 or
specialsales@sterlingpublishing.com.

Manufactured in Canada

2   4   6   8   10   9   7   5   3   1

www.puzzlewright.com

CONTENTS

Introduction
5

Tests

Answers
103

INTRODUCTION

This book of logic puzzles is different from others, and here's why: A typical logic puzzle has only one right answer, and your job is to use the clues to deduce that answer. But in these Logic Games, the clues are only half of the challenge. They provide enough information to limit the number of possible scenarios, but not enough to solve the problem fully.

Then you are given a series of questions asking, for example, which of a given set of scenarios must be true ... or asking which one *could* be true, or perhaps asking which one must be false. Some questions will require you to analyze how different additional circumstances affect the puzzle, narrowing down the set of possible correct scenarios even further. Logic lovers will find that keeping track of the many different possibilities offers a uniquely satisfying challenge not found in most books of logic puzzles.

Besides being fun to solve, these puzzles offer one additional benefit. Ever considered a legal career? This style of logic puzzle is commonly found on entrance exams for law schools. Getting good at them can help to increase your score on this all-important test. (To simulate the test-taking experience, try solving each test with a 35-minute time limit.)

I hope you enjoy these Logic Games as much as I have enjoyed crafting them.

Happy solving!

—Mark Zegarelli

LOGIC GAME 1

Four people—H, J, K, and L—have apartments in the same four-story building. Each person lives on a different floor, from the first floor up to the fourth floor. The following restrictions apply:

- Either H or K lives on the first floor.
- J lives on the floor directly below L.

1. Which of the following could be a list of the four people in order from the first floor up to the fourth floor?

   (A) H, K, L, J
   (B) H, J, K, L
   (C) J, L, K, H
   (D) K, H, J, L
   (E) K, J, H, L

2. Which of the following statements CANNOT be true?

   (A) H lives on the first floor.
   (B) H lives on the second floor.
   (C) J lives on the second floor.
   (D) K lives on the third floor.
   (E) L lives on the fourth floor.

3. If K lives on the second floor, all of the following statements are true EXCEPT:

   (A) H does not live on the third floor.
   (B) H does not live on the fourth floor.
   (C) J does not live on the third floor.
   (D) J does not live on the first floor.
   (E) L does not live on the third floor.

4. If L lives on the third floor, which of the following statements must be true?

(A) H does not live on the first floor.
(B) J does not live on the first floor.
(C) J does not live on the second floor.
(D) K does not live on the first floor.
(E) K does not live on the fourth floor.

5. If J and K live on adjacent floors, which of the following statements must be true?

(A) H lives on either the first floor or the fourth floor.
(B) J lives on either the second floor or the fourth floor.
(C) J lives on either the third floor or the fourth floor.
(D) K lives on either the first floor or the fourth floor.
(E) K lives on either the second floor or the fourth floor.

GO ON TO THE NEXT PAGE

LOGIC GAME 2

An association of local physicians held an election among five members—a dermatologist, a gynecologist, an oncologist, a psychiatrist, and a surgeon. The two physicians who received the most votes became co-presidents of the association. The following information about the results holds true:

- Either the gynecologist or the psychiatrist, but not both, was elected.
- If the gynecologist was not elected, then neither was the dermatologist.
- If the oncologist was not elected, then neither was the psychiatrist.

6. Which of the following could be a complete listing of the doctors who were and were not elected?

(A) elected: dermatologist, oncologist
    not elected: gynecologist, psychiatrist, surgeon
(B) elected: dermatologist, psychiatrist
    not elected: gynecologist, oncologist, surgeon
(C) elected: dermatologist, surgeon
    not elected: gynecologist, oncologist, psychiatrist
(D) elected: gynecologist, psychiatrist
    not elected: dermatologist, oncologist, surgeon
(E) elected: oncologist, psychiatrist
    not elected: dermatologist, gynecologist, surgeon

7. If the surgeon was elected, which of the following is a pair of doctors NEITHER of whom can have been elected?

(A) the dermatologist and the gynecologist
(B) the dermatologist and the oncologist
(C) the gynecologist and the oncologist
(D) the gynecologist and the psychiatrist
(E) the psychiatrist and the surgeon

8. If the gynecologist was elected, which of the following is a complete list of the other doctors who could have been elected?

(A) oncologist
(B) dermatologist, oncologist
(C) dermatologist, surgeon
(D) oncologist, surgeon
(E) dermatologist, oncologist, surgeon

9. If the surgeon was not elected, which of the following statements must be true?

(A) The dermatologist was elected and the oncologist was not elected.

(B) The gynecologist was elected and the oncologist was not elected.

(C) Either the dermatologist or the oncologist, but not both, was elected.

(D) Either the dermatologist or the psychiatrist, but not both, was elected.

(E) Either the oncologist or the psychiatrist, but not both, was elected.

10. If the oncologist was not elected, all of the following could be true EXCEPT:

(A) The gynecologist was elected and the psychiatrist was not elected.

(B) The gynecologist was elected and the surgeon was not elected.

(C) The surgeon was elected and the dermatologist was not elected.

(D) Both the gynecologist and the surgeon were elected.

(E) Both the dermatologist and the surgeon were elected.

11. Which of the following statements must be true?

(A) Either the dermatologist or the surgeon, or both, must have been elected.

(B) Either the gynecologist or the oncologist, or both, must have been elected.

(C) Either the gynecologist or the surgeon, or both, must have been elected.

(D) Either the oncologist or the psychiatrist, or both, must have been elected.

(E) Either the oncologist or the surgeon, or both, must have been elected.

GO ON TO THE NEXT PAGE

LOGIC GAME 3

Two women named Martina and Norah and three men named Oscar, Philip, and Robert all have different zodiac signs—Gemini, Libra, Scorpio, Taurus, and Virgo. The following conditions apply:

- The Libra is a woman.
- The Scorpio is a man.
- Either Norah or Philip is the Taurus.
- Oscar's sign is either Gemini or Virgo.

12. Which of the following could be a complete listing of each person's zodiac sign?

(A) Martina, Libra; Norah, Taurus; Oscar, Scorpio; Philip, Virgo; Robert, Gemini

(B) Martina, Libra; Norah, Taurus; Oscar, Virgo; Philip, Gemini; Robert, Scorpio

(C) Martina, Scorpio; Norah, Libra; Oscar, Virgo; Philip, Taurus; Robert, Gemini

(D) Martina, Taurus; Norah, Libra; Oscar, Gemini; Philip, Scorpio; Robert, Virgo

(E) Martina, Virgo; Norah, Taurus; Oscar, Gemini; Philip, Scorpio; Robert, Libra

13. If Philip's sign is Scorpio, which of the following statements must be true?

(A) Martina's sign is Libra.
(B) Norah's sign is Gemini.
(C) Norah's sign is Libra.
(D) Robert's sign is Taurus.
(E) Robert's sign is Virgo.

14. If Robert's sign is Virgo, which of the following is a complete list of the zodiac signs that could belong to Norah?

(A) Libra
(B) Taurus
(C) Gemini, Taurus
(D) Libra, Taurus
(E) Gemini, Libra, Taurus

15. If Martina's sign is Gemini, all of the following are true EXCEPT:

(A) Norah's sign is not Taurus.
(B) Philip's sign is not Virgo.
(C) Philip's sign is not Scorpio.
(D) Robert's sign is not Scorpio.
(E) Robert's sign is not Virgo.

16. If Norah's sign is neither Libra nor Taurus, which of the following statements must be true?

(A) Norah's sign is Gemini.
(B) Oscar's sign is Gemini.
(C) Oscar's sign is Virgo.
(D) Robert's sign is Scorpio.
(E) Robert's sign is Virgo.

17. If the Gemini is a woman, how many of the five people's signs can be determined?

(A) 0
(B) 1
(C) 2
(D) 3
(E) 5

GO ON TO THE NEXT PAGE

LOGIC GAME 4

A display with three shelves—a top shelf, a middle shelf, and a bottom shelf—has six items displayed on it: a decorative box, a football trophy, a lava lamp, a photograph, a stuffed animal, and a vase. Each shelf has exactly two items, in accordance with the following rules:

- The decorative box and the football trophy are on different shelves.
- The lava lamp is on the shelf directly above the stuffed animal.
- The photograph is on a shelf somewhere above the vase.

18. Which of the following could be a complete list of where all six items are located?

(A) top: decorative box, vase
middle: lava lamp, photograph
bottom: football trophy, stuffed animal

(B) top: football trophy, lava lamp
middle: photograph, stuffed animal
bottom: decorative box, vase

(C) top: lava lamp, photograph
middle: decorative box, vase
bottom: football trophy, stuffed animal

(D) top: lava lamp, photograph
middle: stuffed animal, vase
bottom: decorative box, football trophy

(E) top: photograph, vase
middle: football trophy, lava lamp
bottom: decorative box, stuffed animal

19. If the photograph is on the middle shelf, which of the following statements must be true?

(A) The decorative box is on the bottom shelf.
(B) The football trophy is on the top shelf.
(C) The lava lamp is on the top shelf.
(D) The stuffed animal is on the bottom shelf.
(E) The vase is on the middle shelf.

20. If the vase is on the middle shelf, which of the following two items must be on the same shelf?

(A) the decorative box and the photograph
(B) the football trophy and the stuffed animal
(C) the lava lamp and the photograph
(D) the lava lamp and the vase
(E) the stuffed animal and the vase

21. If the football trophy is on the middle shelf, which of the following statements must be true?

(A) The decorative box is on the top shelf.
(B) The lava lamp is on the middle shelf.
(C) The photograph is on the middle shelf.
(D) The stuffed animal is on the bottom shelf.
(E) The vase is on the bottom shelf.

22. If the decorative box is on the bottom shelf, which of the following is a complete list of the items that could be on the same shelf as the lava lamp?

(A) football trophy, photograph
(B) football trophy, vase
(C) photograph, stuffed animal
(D) football trophy, photograph, stuffed animal
(E) football trophy, photograph, vase

23. If the football trophy and the stuffed animal are on the same shelf, each of the following statements could be true EXCEPT:

(A) The decorative box is on the middle shelf.
(B) The lava lamp is on the top shelf.
(C) The lava lamp is on the middle shelf.
(D) The photograph is on the top shelf.
(E) The vase is on the bottom shelf.

STOP

If you finish before time is up, you may check your work.
Solutions are on pages 104–105.

LOGIC GAME 1

Four people—Raymond, Samantha, Tyler, and Ursula—were interviewed for a job. All four people were interviewed one after the other, with no two interviewed at the same time.

- Either Raymond or Samantha was interviewed third.
- Tyler was interviewed sometime before Ursula.

1. Which of the following could be the order in which the four people were interviewed?

    (A) Raymond, Ursula, Samantha, Tyler
    (B) Samantha, Tyler, Ursula, Raymond
    (C) Samantha, Raymond, Tyler, Ursula
    (D) Tyler, Samantha, Raymond, Ursula
    (E) Ursula, Tyler, Raymond, Samantha

2. Which of the following CANNOT be true?

    (A) Raymond was interviewed first and Samantha was interviewed third.
    (B) Raymond was interviewed second and Samantha was interviewed third.
    (C) Samantha was interviewed second and Ursula was interviewed fourth.
    (D) Tyler was interviewed first and Raymond was interviewed fourth.
    (E) Tyler was interviewed second and Samantha was interviewed fourth.

3. Which of the following must be true?

(A) If Raymond was interviewed first, then Ursula was interviewed fourth.
(B) If Samantha was interviewed first, then Tyler was interviewed third.
(C) If Tyler was interviewed first, then Raymond was interviewed fourth.
(D) If Tyler was interviewed second, then Raymond was interviewed third.
(E) If Ursula was interviewed second, then Samantha was interviewed fourth.

4. If Samantha was interviewed second, which of the following must be true?

(A) Raymond was interviewed immediately before Samantha.
(B) Raymond was interviewed immediately before Ursula.
(C) Samantha was interviewed immediately before Tyler.
(D) Tyler was interviewed immediately before Raymond.
(E) Ursula was interviewed immediately before Raymond.

5. If Ursula was NOT interviewed fourth, which of the following could be true?

(A) Raymond was interviewed first.
(B) Raymond was interviewed second.
(C) Samantha was interviewed second
(D) Samantha was interviewed fourth.
(E) Tyler was interviewed second.

GO ON TO THE NEXT PAGE

LOGIC GAME 2

Four people named Forbes, Gorman, Halliwell, and Ivorsen are playing bridge, seated around a square table at four positions located at the North, East, South, and West sides of the table.

- The pair seated North and South are partners, as are the pair seated East and West.
- Forbes and Ivorsen are not partners.
- Halliwell is seated either North or East.

6. Which of the following is a possible listing of each person's position?

(A) North: Forbes; East: Gorman; South: Halliwell; West: Ivorsen

(B) North: Forbes; East: Gorman; South: Ivorsen; West: Halliwell

(C) North: Gorman; East: Halliwell; South: Ivorsen; West: Forbes

(D) North: Halliwell; East: Forbes; South: Gorman; West: Ivorsen

(E) North: Ivorsen; East: Gorman; South: Halliwell; West: Forbes

7. If Forbes is seated North, which of the following is a complete list of the people who could be seated South?

(A) Gorman

(B) Halliwell

(C) Gorman and Halliwell

(D) Gorman and Ivorsen

(E) Gorman, Halliwell, and Ivorsen

8. Which of the following statements CANNOT be true?

(A) Forbes and Gorman are partners.

(B) Forbes and Halliwell are partners.

(C) Gorman and Halliwell are partners.

(D) Gorman and Ivorsen are partners.

(E) Halliwell and Ivorsen are partners.

9. If Gorman is seated West, which of the following statements must be true?

(A) Forbes is not seated East.
(B) Forbes is not seated South.
(C) Halliwell is not seated North.
(D) Ivorsen is not seated North.
(E) Ivorsen is not seated East.

10. If Forbes and Gorman are not partners, which of the following statements must be FALSE?

(A) Forbes and Halliwell are partners.
(B) Gorman and Halliwell are not partners.
(C) Gorman and Ivorsen are not partners.
(D) Forbes is seated South.
(E) Ivorsen is seated East.

11. If Ivorsen is seated West, which of the following is a complete listing of the positions where Forbes could be seated but where Halliwell CANNOT be seated?

(A) North
(B) South
(C) North and East
(D) North and South
(E) East and South

GO ON TO THE NEXT PAGE

LOGIC GAME 3

Three delegates are selected from a group of six nominees—J, K, L, M, N, and O—to represent their organization at a national gathering.

- If J is selected, then L is not selected.
- Either K and N are both selected or both not selected.
- O is selected only if M is also selected.

12. Which of the following pairs of people CANNOT both be selected?

(A) J and K
(B) K and L
(C) L and M
(D) M and N
(E) N and O

13. If neither J nor M is selected as a delegate, which of the following CANNOT be selected?

(A) K
(B) L
(C) N
(D) O
(E) Any of these people could be selected.

14. Which of the following statements could be FALSE?

(A) If J and K are both selected, then N is also selected.
(B) If L and M are both selected, then O is also selected.
(C) If L and N are both selected, then K is also selected.
(D) If M and N are both selected, then K is also selected.
(E) If M and O are both selected, then L is also selected.

15. If L is selected but K is not selected, which of the following statements could be FALSE?

(A) J is not selected.
(B) M is selected.
(C) N is not selected.
(D) O is selected.
(E) none of the above

16. If K is selected but L is not selected, which of the following statements could be true?

(A) J is selected but N is not selected.
(B) M is selected but N is not selected.
(C) N is selected but J is not selected.
(D) O is selected but L is not selected.
(E) O is selected but M is not selected.

17. Which of the following statements must be true?

(A) If J is selected, then M is not selected.
(B) If K is selected, then M is not selected.
(C) If K is selected, then O is not selected.
(D) If L is selected, then K is selected.
(E) If M is selected, then O is selected.

GO ON TO THE NEXT PAGE

LOGIC GAME 4

Each of five people—V, W, X, Y, and Z—has chosen to visit Italy, Japan, or Kenya for his or her next vacation. Each person will visit exactly one of the three countries, and at least one of the five will visit each country, according to the following conditions:

- V will not visit Italy.
- V and W will visit the same country.
- W and X will visit different countries.
- Either Y and Z will both visit Kenya, or Y will visit Italy and Z will visit Japan.

18. Which of the following is a possible itinerary for the five people?

(A) Italy: X	Japan: W	Kenya: V, Y, and Z
(B) Italy: Y	Japan: X and Z	Kenya: V and W
(C) Italy: Y	Japan: Z	Kenya: V, W, and X
(D) Italy: X and Z	Japan: Y	Kenya: V and W
(E) Italy: V, W, and Y	Japan: Z	Kenya: X

19. If Z is the only person who visits Japan, which of the following is a complete list of the people who could visit Kenya?

(A) X
(B) Y
(C) V and W
(D) X and Y
(E) V, W, and X

20. If at least one person other than Y (but not necessarily Y) visits Italy, which of the following pairs of people could travel to the same country?

(A) V and X
(B) W and Y
(C) W and Z
(D) X and Z
(E) Y and Z

21. If three people visit one of the countries, which of the following statements must be true?

(A) X is the only person who visits Italy.
(B) X is the only person who visits Japan.
(C) Y is the only person who visits Italy.
(D) Z is the only person who visits Japan.
(E) Z is the only person who visits Kenya.

22. If X visits Japan, which of the following statements must be true?

(A) X is the only person who visits Japan.
(B) Aside from X, Y is the only other person who visits Japan.
(C) Aside from X, Z is the only other person who visits Japan.
(D) Aside from X, V and W are the only other people who visit Japan.
(E) Aside from X, Y and Z are the only other people who visit Japan.

23. Which of the following is a complete listing of the countries that any of the five people could visit, and only those countries?

(A) Italy
(B) Japan
(C) Kenya
(D) Japan and Kenya
(E) None of the three countries could be visited by any of the five people.

STOP

If you finish before time is up, you may check your work.
Solutions are on pages 106–107.

LOGIC GAME 1

Five people named Hong, Jarvis, Klein, Lofford, and Nettis are deciding whether to attend a Broadway play, based on the following restrictions:

- At least two of the five people attend the play.
- Jarvis and Klein will either both attend or both not attend.
- Hong will attend if and only if Lofford does not attend.
- If Nettis attends, then Klein does not attend.

1. Which of the following could be a complete list of the people who do and do not attend the play?

   (A) attend: Hong, Jarvis, Klein, Nettis
       do not attend: Lofford
   (B) attend: Jarvis, Klein
       do not attend: Hong, Lofford, Nettis
   (C) attend: Klein, Lofford
       do not attend: Hong, Jarvis, Nettis
   (D) attend: Lofford
       do not attend: Hong, Jarvis, Klein, and Nettis
   (E) attend: Lofford, Nettis
       do not attend: Hong, Jarvis, Klein

2. Which of the following pairs of people could not both attend the play?

   (A) Hong and Jarvis
   (B) Hong and Nettis
   (C) Jarvis and Lofford
   (D) Jarvis and Nettis
   (E) Klein and Lofford

3. If Nettis does not attend the play, which of the following is a complete list of the people who must attend?

   (A) Hong
   (B) Lofford
   (C) Jarvis and Klein
   (D) Hong, Jarvis, and Klein
   (E) Jarvis, Klein, and Lofford

4. If Hong attends the play and Lofford does not, which of the following is a complete list of the people who CANNOT attend it?

(A) Lofford
(B) Klein and Lofford
(C) Lofford and Nettis
(D) Jarvis, Klein, and Lofford
(E) Jarvis, Klein, Lofford, and Nettis

5. If exactly two people attend the play, which of the following statements must be true?

(A) Hong attends the play and Klein does not.
(B) Nettis attends the play and Jarvis does not.
(C) Neither Hong nor Lofford attends the play.
(D) Neither Hong nor Jarvis attends the play.
(E) Neither Klein nor Lofford attends the play.

6. If Jarvis attends the play, which of the following statements must be true?

(A) Exactly two people must attend the play.
(B) Exactly three people must attend the play.
(C) Exactly four people must attend the play.
(D) Either two or three people could attend the play.
(E) Either three or four people could attend the play.

GO ON TO THE NEXT PAGE

LOGIC GAME 2

Five people—two women named Grace and Maria, and three men named William, Xavier, and Zachary—order individual pizzas. Each person orders exactly one of five toppings—anchovies, chicken, olives, peppers, or sausage—and exactly one person orders each topping, according to the following conditions:

- A woman orders the pizza with chicken.
- A man orders the pizza with the peppers.
- Either Grace or William orders the pizza with the sausage.
- Xavier orders either the anchovies or the olives.

7. Which of the following statements must be true?

(A) Maria orders either the chicken or the olives.
(B) William orders either the anchovies or the peppers.
(C) Either Grace or Xavier orders the olives.
(D) Either William or Xavier orders the anchovies.
(E) Either William or Zachary orders the peppers.

8. If Maria doesn't order the chicken, which of the following statements must be FALSE?

(A) Grace orders the chicken.
(B) William orders the sausage.
(C) Xavier orders the anchovies.
(D) Xavier orders the olives.
(E) Zachary orders the anchovies.

9. If Grace orders the anchovies, which of the following statements must be true?

(A) Maria orders the chicken but William doesn't order the peppers.
(B) Maria orders the chicken but Xavier doesn't order the olives.
(C) William orders the sausage but Maria doesn't order the chicken.
(D) Zachary orders the sausage but William doesn't order the olives.
(E) Zachary orders the peppers but Xavier doesn't order the olives.

10. If a woman orders the olives, how many people's orders are determined?

(A) 0
(B) 1
(C) 2
(D) 3
(E) 5

11. If William orders neither the peppers nor the sausage, how many people's orders are determined?

(A) 0
(B) 1
(C) 2
(D) 3
(E) 5

GO ON TO THE NEXT PAGE

LOGIC GAME 3

Five people—Lana, Matt, Nora, Oliver, and Paula—stood in line for an event.

- Either Matt or Nora was second in line
- Oliver and Paula stood next to each other.
- If Lana was first in line, then Paula was fifth.

12. Which of the following could be the order in which the five people stood in line?

(A) Lana, Nora, Matt, Paula, Oliver
(B) Matt, Nora, Oliver, Lana, Paula
(C) Matt, Paula, Oliver, Nora, Lana
(D) Nora, Matt, Lana, Oliver, Paula
(E) Nora, Lana, Paula, Oliver, Matt

13. If Lana was first in line, which of the following is a complete list of the people who could have been third?

(A) Matt
(B) Nora
(C) Matt and Nora
(D) Matt, Nora, and Oliver
(E) Matt, Nora, Oliver, and Paula

14. If Matt and Paula stood next to each other, which of the following must be FALSE?

(A) Lana stood directly in front of Nora.
(B) Matt stood directly in front of Paula.
(C) Nora stood directly in front of Matt.
(D) Oliver stood directly in front of Lana.
(E) Paula stood directly in front of Oliver.

15. If Matt was second in line, which of the following pairs of people could NOT have stood next to each other?

(A) Lana and Matt
(B) Lana and Paula
(C) Matt and Oliver
(D) Nora and Oliver
(E) Nora and Paula

16. If Oliver was not fourth in line, which of the following statements could be true?

(A) Lana was first in line.
(B) Matt was third in line.
(C) Paula was third in line.
(D) Lana was fifth in line.
(E) Nora was fifth in line.

17. Which of the following is a complete list of the people who could have been third in line?

(A) Lana, Matt, and Nora
(B) Lana, Oliver, and Paula
(C) Lana, Matt, Nora, and Oliver
(D) Lana, Matt, Nora, and Paula
(E) Lana, Matt, Nora, Oliver, and Paula

GO ON TO THE NEXT PAGE

LOGIC GAME 4

Main Street runs from north to south, with odd-numbered houses on the west side of the street and even-numbered houses on the east side. House numbers increase from north to south. Houses #1 and #2 are directly across from each other, as are houses #3 and #4, and #5 and #6. The owners of these six houses are, in some order, Q, R, S, T, U, and V.

- Either Q or V lives in House #1.
- S and T live directly across from each other.
- R and V live on the same side of the street in adjacent houses.

18. Which of the following could be a complete listing of each house and its owner?

(A) #1: Q #2: U
    #3: T #4: S
    #5: V #6: R

(B) #1: Q #2: R
    #3: U #4: V
    #5: S #6: T

(C) #1: T #2: S
    #3: R #4: Q
    #5: V #6: U

(D) #1: V #2: Q
    #3: R #4: T
    #5: S #6: U

(E) #1: V #2: R
    #3: U #4: Q
    #5: S #6: T

19. Which of the following pairs of people could not live on the same side of the street in adjacent houses?

(A) Q and U
(B) R and V
(C) S and U
(D) T and V
(E) U and V

20. Which of the following is a complete list of the people who could own #3?

(A) R and U
(B) Q, R, and U
(C) R, U, and V
(D) Q, R, U, and V
(E) R, S, T, and U

21. Which of the following people must live on the same side of the street?

(A) Q and U
(B) Q and S
(C) R and S
(D) S and V
(E) T and U

22. If R and T live on opposite sides of the street, which of the following CANNOT be true?

(A) Q and T live on the same side of the street.
(B) Q and U live on the same side of the street.
(C) S and V live on the same side of the street.
(D) R and U live on opposite sides of the street.
(E) T and U live on opposite sides of the street.

23. If T and U live on the same side of the street in adjacent houses, which of the following could be FALSE?

(A) Q lives in either #1 or #2.
(B) R lives in either #3 or #4.
(C) U lives in either #3 or #4.
(D) S lives in either #5 or #6.
(E) T lives in either #5 or #6.

STOP

If you finish before time is up, you may check your work.
Solutions are on pages 108–109.

LOGIC GAME 1

Five men, each wearing a different type of hat, are standing in a straight line waiting for a movie. They are wearing a baseball cap, a fedora, a Panama hat, a ski cap, and a ten-gallon hat.

- The man wearing the ski cap is standing two places ahead of the man wearing the baseball cap.
- The man wearing the Panama hat is standing someplace ahead of the man wearing the fedora.
- The man wearing the ten-gallon hat is not third or fourth in line.

1. If the man wearing the Panama hat is third in line, which of the following must be true?

   (A) The man in the ten-gallon hat is first.
   (B) The man in the ski cap hat is first.
   (C) The man in the baseball cap is second.
   (D) The man in the fedora is fourth.
   (E) The man in the ski cap is fourth.

2. If the man wearing the Panama hat is second in line, which of the following could be true?

   (A) The man in the baseball cap is first.
   (B) The man in the fedora is first.
   (C) The man in the fedora is third.
   (D) The man in the ski cap is third.
   (E) The man in the fedora is fifth.

3. Which of the following pairs of men CANNOT be second and third in line, in either order?

   (A) the men in the baseball cap and the Panama hat
   (B) the men in the baseball cap and the ten-gallon hat
   (C) the men in the fedora and the ski cap
   (D) the men in the Panama hat and the ten-gallon hat
   (E) the men in the ski cap and the ten-gallon hat

4. If the man wearing the fedora is NOT fourth in line, all of the following could be true EXCEPT:

(A) The man wearing the Panama hat is first.
(B) The man wearing the ten-gallon hat is second.
(C) The man wearing the ski cap is third.
(D) The man wearing the baseball cap is fourth.
(E) The man wearing the fedora is fifth.

5. If the man wearing the baseball cap is third in line, which of the following pairs of men CANNOT be standing next to each other?

(A) the men in the baseball cap and the fedora
(B) the men in the baseball cap and the Panama hat
(C) the men in the baseball cap and the ten-gallon hat
(D) the men in the fedora and the ski cap
(E) the men in the Panama hat and the ski cap

6. If the men wearing the Panama hat and the ski cap are NOT standing next to each other, which of the following must be true?

(A) The man wearing the ski cap is first.
(B) The man wearing the ten-gallon hat is second.
(C) The man wearing the baseball cap is third.
(D) The man wearing the Panama hat is fourth.
(E) The man wearing the fedora is fifth.

GO ON TO THE NEXT PAGE

LOGIC GAME 2

Three high schools—Hayes, Jackson, and Lincoln—each have two school colors from among the following six colors: black, gold, purple, red, white, and yellow. No two schools have any color in common.

- Hayes does not include black or purple.
- No school has gold and yellow as its two colors.
- No school has purple and red as its two colors.
- If red is one of Lincoln's colors, then gold is one of Hayes's colors; otherwise, Jackson's colors are purple and white.

7. Which of the following could be a complete list of colors for all three schools?

(A) Hayes: black and red
Jackson: purple and white
Lincoln: gold and yellow

(B) Hayes: gold and white
Jackson: purple and yellow
Lincoln: black and red

(C) Hayes: gold and white
Jackson: black and yellow
Lincoln: purple and red

(D) Hayes: gold and yellow
Jackson: purple and white
Lincoln: black and red

(E) Hayes: white and yellow
Jackson: gold and purple
Lincoln: red and black

8. Which of the following statements must be FALSE?

(A) One of Hayes's colors is red.
(B) One of Hayes's colors is yellow.
(C) One of Jackson's colors is black.
(D) One of Jackson's colors is gold.
(E) One of Lincoln's colors is red.

9. If one of Jackson's colors is black, which of the following statements must be true?

(A) One of Hayes's colors is gold.
(B) One of Hayes's colors is red.
(C) One of Lincoln's colors is gold.
(D) One of Lincoln's colors is purple.
(E) One of Lincoln's colors is white.

10. If one school's colors are red and yellow, which of the following statements must be true?

(A) One of Hayes's colors is gold.
(B) One of Jackson's colors is purple.
(C) One of Jackson's colors is white.
(D) One of Lincoln's colors is gold.
(E) One of Lincoln's colors is red.

11. If Jackson's colors do not include white, which of the following statements must be true?

(A) One of Hayes's colors is white and one of Jackson's is black.
(B) One of Hayes's colors is gold and one of Lincoln's is red.
(C) One of Hayes's colors is white and one of Lincoln's is yellow.
(D) One of Jackson's colors is purple and one of Lincoln's is yellow.
(E) One of Jackson's colors is yellow and one of Lincoln's is red.

12. If one of Hayes's colors is red, which of the following is a complete list of the high schools whose colors are determined?

(A) Hayes
(B) Jackson
(C) Lincoln
(D) Hayes, Jackson, and Lincoln
(E) No high school's colors are determined.

13. Which of the following is a complete list of the colors that could be among those chosen by any of the three schools?

(A) white
(B) yellow
(C) gold and white
(D) gold and yellow
(E) white and yellow

GO ON TO THE NEXT PAGE

LOGIC GAME 3

A group of exactly three students are selected to represent a group that contains seven senior members—D, E, F, G, H, J, and K. The following conditions hold:

- D is selected if and only if G is not selected.
- If G is selected, then H is also selected.
- J and K are either both selected or both not selected.
- If J is not selected, then F is selected.

14. Which of the following could be a complete listing of the three students who were selected and the four students who were not chosen?

    (A) selected: D, E, and H
        not selected: F, G, J, and K
    (B) selected: D, E, and J
        not selected: F, G, H, and K
    (C) selected: D, J, and K
        not selected: E, F, G, and H
    (D) selected: F, J, and K
        not selected: D, E, G, and H
    (E) selected: G, J, and K
        not selected: D, E, F, and H

15. If F is not selected, which of the following pairs of people must be selected?

    (A) D and H
    (B) D and J
    (C) E and K
    (D) E and J
    (E) H and K

16. If G is selected, which of the following pairs of people must NOT be selected?

(A) D and F
(B) D and H
(C) E and J
(D) F and J
(E) H and K

17. If K is not selected, which of the following statements must be true?

(A) D is selected and H is not selected.
(B) D is selected and J is not selected.
(C) F is selected and E is not selected.
(D) F is selected and J is not selected.
(E) G is selected and E is not selected.

18. Which of the following pairs of people could both be selected?

(A) D and K
(B) E and G
(C) E and H
(D) G and J
(E) H and K

GO ON TO THE NEXT PAGE

LOGIC GAME 4

A six-story apartment building has exactly one unit on each of its six floors, from the first floor, which is lowest, to the sixth floor, which is highest.

- No pair of consecutive floors are both rented.
- Among the lowest three floors, at least one is rented.
- Among the top four floors, at least two are rented.

19. Which of the following is a complete list of how many floors could be rented?

(A) 2
(B) 3
(C) 4
(D) 2 or 3
(E) 2, 3, or 4

20. If the first and fourth floors are both rented, which of the following statements must be true?

(A) The second floor is rented and the third floor is not rented.
(B) The second floor is not rented and fifth floor is rented.
(C) The second and fifth floors are both not rented.
(D) The second and sixth floors are both rented.
(E) The third and sixth floors are both not rented.

21. If the sixth floor is not rented, which of the following is a complete list of the floors that must be rented?

(A) first and third
(B) first and fourth
(C) first and fifth
(D) third and fifth
(E) first, third, and fifth

22. Which of the following is a pair of consecutive floors that could both be NOT rented?

(A) No pair of consecutive floors could both be not rented.
(B) the first and second floors
(C) the third and fourth floors
(D) the fifth and sixth floors
(E) Any pair of consecutive floors could both be not rented.

23. Which of the following conditions determines whether all six apartments are rented or not rented?

(A) if the second floor is rented
(B) if the third floor is not rented
(C) if the fourth floor is rented
(D) if the fifth floor is rented
(E) if the sixth floor is not rented

STOP

If you finish before time is up, you may check your work.
Solutions are on pages 110–111.

LOGIC GAME 1

Jane made six trips to six cities in Europe—Lisbon, Madrid, Oslo, Prague, Rome, and Stockholm—in 2011, 2012, and 2013. In each year, she made one trip in the spring and another in the fall, according to the following conditions:

- She visited Stockholm in the fall and Madrid the following spring.
- She visited Lisbon sometime before she visited Prague.
- She visited Oslo sometime before she visited Rome.

1. Which of the following could be a complete listing of the six cities that Jane visited in the order that she visited them?

    (A) Lisbon, Rome, Oslo, Stockholm, Madrid, Prague
    (B) Lisbon, Stockholm, Madrid, Prague, Rome, Oslo
    (C) Oslo, Lisbon, Rome, Stockholm, Madrid, Prague
    (D) Oslo, Rome, Stockholm, Madrid, Lisbon, Prague
    (E) Oslo, Stockholm, Madrid, Prague, Lisbon, Rome

2. If Jane visited Rome in the fall of 2011, which city did she visit in the spring of 2012?

    (A) Lisbon
    (B) Madrid
    (C) Oslo
    (D) Prague
    (E) Stockholm

3. If Jane visited Prague in the spring of 2012, which of the following pairs of cities must she have visited during the same year?

    (A) Lisbon and Oslo
    (B) Lisbon and Madrid
    (C) Oslo and Prague
    (D) Prague and Rome
    (E) Rome and Stockholm

4. If Jane visited Rome in the fall of 2012, which of the following is the list of the three cities that she visited in spring, in the order in which she visited them?

    (A) Lisbon, Madrid, Oslo
    (B) Madrid, Lisbon, Oslo
    (C) Madrid, Lisbon, Prague
    (D) Oslo, Madrid, Lisbon
    (E) Oslo, Prague, Lisbon

5. If Jane visited Prague in 2012, which of the following is a complete list of the cities that she could have visited in the fall of 2011?

    (A) Lisbon
    (B) Stockholm
    (C) Lisbon and Oslo
    (D) Oslo and Stockholm
    (E) Lisbon, Oslo, and Stockholm

6. If Jane visited Lisbon during a fall trip, then she could have visited each of the following pairs of cities in the same year as each other EXCEPT:

    (A) Madrid and Oslo
    (B) Madrid and Prague
    (C) Madrid and Rome
    (D) Oslo and Stockholm
    (E) Prague and Rome

GO ON TO THE NEXT PAGE

LOGIC GAME 2

A family has seven children—four boys named Scott, Tyrone, Victor, and Wally, and three girls named Iris, Jasmine, and Kaylie. Exactly three children cook dinner on Sunday nights, according to the following restrictions:

- At least one boy and at least one girl always cooks.
- Either Scott or Kaylie always cooks, but never together.
- If Tyrone cooks, then Victor also cooks.
- If Iris cooks, then neither Jasmine nor Scott cooks.

7. Which of the following could be a complete list of who cooks and who doesn't?

(A) cooks: Iris, Kaylie, Tyrone
   doesn't cook: Jasmine, Scott, Victor, Wally
(B) cooks: Scott, Tyrone, Victor
   doesn't cook: Iris, Jasmine, Kaylie, Wally
(C) cooks: Iris, Scott, Wally
   doesn't cook: Jasmine, Kaylie, Tyrone, Victor
(D) cooks: Iris, Victor, Wally
   doesn't cook: Jasmine, Kaylie, Scott, Tyrone
(E) cooks: Jasmine, Scott, Wally
   doesn't cook: Iris, Kaylie, Tyrone, Victor

8. If Iris cooks, which of the following pairs of children must NOT cook?

(A) Jasmine and Kaylie
(B) Jasmine and Tyrone
(C) Jasmine and Victor
(D) Scott and Victor
(E) Tyrone and Wally

9. If both Victor and Wally cook, which of the following statements must be true?

(A) Iris cooks.
(B) Jasmine cooks.
(C) Kaylie cooks.
(D) Scott cooks.
(E) Tyrone cooks.

10. If Wally doesn't cook, which of the following children must cook?

(A) Iris
(B) Jasmine
(C) Kaylie
(D) Scott
(E) Victor

11. If Victor cooks but Kaylie doesn't cook, which of the following statements must be true?

(A) Iris and Scott both cook.
(B) Jasmine and Scott both cook.
(C) Neither Iris nor Scott cooks.
(D) Neither Jasmine nor Wally cooks.
(E) Neither Scott nor Tyrone cooks.

12. If two of the girls cook, which of the following statements must be true?

(A) Neither Scott nor Tyrone cooks.
(B) Neither Scott nor Victor cooks.
(C) Neither Scott nor Wally cooks.
(D) Neither Tyrone nor Victor cooks.
(E) Neither Tyrone nor Wally cooks.

13. Which of the following statements must be FALSE?

(A) Iris cooks with two of her brothers.
(B) Jasmine cooks with two of her brothers.
(C) Kaylie cooks with two of her brothers.
(D) Victor cooks with two of his sisters.
(E) Wally cooks with two of his sisters.

GO ON TO THE NEXT PAGE

LOGIC GAME 3

Alicia's morning routine always includes at least one set each of glute crunches, leg lifts, push-ups, and squats. She does five minutes of exercises, with each minute dedicated to one of these four exercises, subject to the following conditions.

- She never repeats the same exercise for two consecutive minutes.
- Her first minute is always either push-ups or squats.
- She never immediately follows leg lifts with glute crunches.
- She never immediately follows push-ups with squats.
- She never immediately follows squats with leg lifts.

14. Which of the following could be a list of the five exercises that Alicia does in the order in which she does them?

(A) push-ups, glute crunches, leg lifts, squats, leg lifts
(B) push-ups, leg lifts, glute crunches, squats, push-ups
(C) push-ups, squats, push-ups, glute crunches, leg lifts
(D) squats, glute crunches, push-ups, glute crunches, squats
(E) squats, push-ups, leg lifts, push-ups, glute crunches

15. If Alicia's third set is glute crunches, each of the following statements could be true EXCEPT:

(A) Her first set is squats.
(B) Her second set is push-ups.
(C) Her fourth set is leg lifts.
(D) Her fourth set is push-ups.
(E) Her fifth set is glute crunches.

16. If Alicia's fourth set is leg lifts, which of the following statements must be true?

(A) Either her first or second set is push-ups.
(B) Either her first or second set is squats.
(C) Either her second or third set is glute crunches.
(D) Either her second or third set is squats.
(E) Either her third or fifth set is push-ups.

42

17. If Alicia does two sets of glute crunches, which of the following statements must be true?

(A) Either her first or third set is squats.
(B) Either her first or fourth set is push-ups.
(C) Either her second or third set is leg lifts.
(D) Either her third or fourth set is push-ups.
(E) Either her third or fifth set is leg lifts.

18. If Alicia's first and fifth sets are both push-ups, each of the following statements could be true EXCEPT:

(A) Her second set is glute crunches.
(B) Her second set is leg lifts.
(C) Her third set is glute crunches.
(D) Her third set is leg lifts.
(E) Her fourth set is glute crunches.

GO ON TO THE NEXT PAGE

LOGIC GAME 4

Main Street runs from north to south, crossing Sunset Avenue, which runs from west to east. At this intersection lie four restaurants, each specializing in a different type of food—French, Greek, Italian, or Japanese—and each owned by a different person, surnamed Thomsen, Ulrich, Valencia, or Wilton.

- Either Ulrich or Wilton owns the restaurant at the northwest corner.
- The restaurant at the northeast corner serves either Greek or Italian food.
- Thomsen's restaurant and the French restaurant are both on the same side of Sunset Avenue.
- Valencia's restaurant and the Japanese restaurant are on the same side of Main Street.

19. Which of the following could be a complete listing of the four restaurants by location, including each restaurant's owner and the type of food it serves?

   (A) northwest: Ulrich, Greek
        northeast: Valencia, Italian
        southwest: Thomsen, Japanese
        southeast: Wilton, French
   (B) northwest: Wilton, Greek
        northeast: Valencia, Italian
        southwest: Ulrich, French
        southeast: Thomsen, Japanese
   (C) northwest: Valencia, Greek
        northeast: Wilton, Italian
        southwest: Thomsen, Japanese
        southeast: Ulrich, French
   (D) northwest: Wilton, Japanese
        northeast: Ulrich, Italian
        southwest: Valencia, Greek
        southeast: Thomsen, French
   (E) northwest: Ulrich, Greek
        northeast: Thomsen, Japanese
        southwest: Wilton, Italian
        southeast: Valencia, French

20. If the Italian restaurant is on the southeast corner, which of the following statements must be true?

(A) Ulrich's restaurant is north of Sunset Avenue.
(B) Ulrich's restaurant is south of Sunset Avenue.
(C) Ulrich's restaurant is east of Main Street.
(D) Ulrich's restaurant is west of Main Street.
(E) none of the above

21. If Thomsen owns the Japanese restaurant, which of the following must be FALSE?

(A) Ulrich owns the French restaurant.
(B) Ulrich owns the Greek restaurant.
(C) Valencia owns the French restaurant.
(D) Valencia owns the Italian restaurant.
(E) Wilton owns the Greek restaurant.

22. If Wilton owns the Italian restaurant, which of the following statements could be true?

(A) Thomsen's Greek restaurant is on the northwest corner.
(B) Thomsen's Japanese restaurant is on the southwest corner.
(C) Ulrich's Japanese restaurant is on the northwest corner.
(D) Ulrich's French restaurant is on the southeast corner.
(E) Valencia's Greek restaurant is on the southwest corner.

23. Which of the following statements must be true?

(A) The French restaurant is on the southwest corner.
(B) The Greek restaurant is on the northwest corner.
(C) The Japanese restaurant is on the southeast corner.
(D) Valencia's restaurant is on the northeast corner.
(E) Wilton's restaurant is on the northwest corner.

STOP

If you finish before time is up, you may check your work.
Solutions are on pages 112–113.

LOGIC GAME 1

A cafeteria offers three types of soup (potato leek, tomato barley, or vegetable), three entrées (ham, linguini, or meatloaf), and three desserts (blueberry pie, chocolate cake, or donut à la mode). Zachary orders a soup, an entrée, and a dessert according to the following restrictions:

- If he orders potato leek soup, then he also orders ham.
- If he orders tomato barley soup, then he also orders chocolate cake.
- If he orders linguini, then he also orders donut à la mode.
- If he orders blueberry pie, then he also orders vegetable soup.

1. Which of the following could be a complete list of the three items that Zachary orders?

(A) potato leek soup, ham, blueberry pie
(B) potato leek soup, meatloaf, donut à la mode
(C) tomato barley soup, linguini, donut à la mode
(D) vegetable soup, linguini, blueberry pie
(E) vegetable soup, meatloaf, chocolate cake

2. If Zachary orders potato leek soup, which of the following is a complete list of the desserts that he could order?

(A) chocolate cake
(B) donut à la mode
(C) blueberry pie, chocolate cake
(D) blueberry pie, donut à la mode
(E) chocolate cake, donut à la mode

3. If Zachary orders the linguini, which of the following is a complete list of the soups he could order?

(A) potato leek
(B) tomato barley
(C) vegetable
(D) potato leek, vegetable
(E) tomato barley, vegetable

4. If Zachary orders the chocolate cake, which of the following statements must be FALSE?

(A) He orders the potato leek soup and the ham.
(B) He orders the tomato barley soup and the ham.
(C) He orders the tomato barley soup and the meatloaf.
(D) He orders the vegetable soup and the linguini.
(E) He orders the vegetable soup and the meatloaf.

5. If Zachary doesn't order donut à la mode, which of the following is a complete list of the soups that he could order?

(A) tomato barley
(B) vegetable
(C) potato leek, vegetable
(D) tomato barley, vegetable
(E) potato leek, tomato barley, vegetable

GO ON TO THE NEXT PAGE

LOGIC GAME 2

A three-story house includes three apartments, one on each floor. Seven people surnamed Granger, Jones, Magyar, Perkins, Roseld, Taylor, and Weld live in the house, with at least two in each apartment, subject to the following conditions:

- Granger lives on the floor directly below Taylor.
- Perkins and Weld live on the same floor.
- Magyar lives on a lower floor than Roseld.
- Jones lives on the third floor.

6. Which of the following could be a complete listing of where all seven people live?

(A) first: Granger, Magyar
  second: Perkins, Weld
  third: Jones, Roseld, Taylor
(B) first: Granger, Magyar
  second: Roseld, Taylor
  third: Jones, Perkins, Weld
(C) first: Granger, Perkins, Weld
  second: Roseld, Taylor
  third: Jones, Magyar
(D) first: Perkins, Weld
  second: Granger, Jones, Magyar
  third: Roseld, Taylor
(E) first: Magyar, Perkins
  second: Granger, Roseld, Weld
  third: Jones, Taylor

7. If Magyar lives on the second floor, which of the following statements must be true?

(A) Granger lives on the second floor.
(B) Perkins lives on the first floor.
(C) Roseld lives on the second floor.
(D) Taylor lives on the second floor.
(E) Taylor lives on the third floor.

8. If three people live on the second floor, which of the following pairs of people must live on the same floor?

(A) Granger and Magyar
(B) Granger and Roseld
(C) Jones and Perkins
(D) Magyar and Weld
(E) Perkins and Roseld

9. If Roseld lives on the third floor with two other people, which of the following statements must be true?

(A) Granger lives on the first floor.
(B) Magyar lives on the second floor.
(C) Perkins lives on the second floor
(D) Taylor lives on the second floor.
(E) Weld lives on the third floor.

10. If Granger and Magyar live on the same floor, which of the following is a complete list of the people who could live with Roseld?

(A) Jones
(B) Taylor
(C) Jones, Taylor
(D) Granger, Jones, Magyar, Taylor
(E) Granger, Jones, Magyar, Perkins, Taylor, Weld

GO ON TO THE NEXT PAGE

LOGIC GAME 3

A company posted rankings for its top six sales employees, including three men (H, J, and K) and three women (M, N, and P).

- The first- and second-ranked employees are of opposite sexes.
- H ranked immediately above K.
- P ranked either fourth or fifth.
- M ranked higher than J.

11. Which of the following could be a complete list of the top six employees in order from highest-ranked to lowest-ranked?

(A) H, K, M, P, J, N
(B) M, H, K, P, J, N
(C) M, J, P, N, H, K
(D) N, H, M, J, P, K
(E) N, J, H, K, P, M

12. If H was ranked fifth, which of the following statements must be FALSE?

(A) J was ranked one position higher than N.
(B) M was ranked one position higher than J.
(C) N was ranked one position higher than P.
(D) M was ranked two positions higher than P.
(E) P was ranked two positions higher than K.

13. Which of the following is a complete list of the employees who could have ranked third?

(A) H, K, N
(B) H, J, K, M
(C) H, J, K, N
(D) H, K, M, N
(E) H, J, K, M, N

14. If M was ranked fourth, which of the following was ranked two positions higher than P?

(A) H
(B) J
(C) K
(D) M
(E) N

15. If N was ranked highest, which of the following statements must be true?

(A) J was ranked fourth.
(B) J was ranked sixth.
(C) M was ranked fourth.
(D) M was ranked fifth.
(E) P was ranked fifth.

16. Which of the following statements must be FALSE?

(A) M was ranked first and J was ranked second.
(B) N was ranked first and J was ranked second.
(C) K was ranked third and P was ranked fourth.
(D) P was ranked fourth and H was ranked fifth.
(E) P was ranked fifth and N was ranked sixth.

17. N could have been ranked any of the following EXCEPT:

(A) first
(B) second
(C) fourth
(D) fifth
(E) sixth

18. If P was ranked fifth, which of the following statements must be FALSE?

(A) H and J had fewer than two employees ranked between them.
(B) H and N had fewer than two employees ranked between them.
(C) J and K had fewer than two employees ranked between them.
(D) J and M had fewer than two employees ranked between them.
(E) M and N had fewer than two employees ranked between them.

GO ON TO THE NEXT PAGE

LOGIC GAME 4

Four students surnamed Vickery, Wade, Young, and Zuckerman play sports on one or more of their high school's three sports teams—baseball, football, and soccer. Each student plays on at least one of these teams, and each team includes at least one of these four players. The following conditions apply:

- Exactly one student plays on all three teams.
- Vickery plays on the baseball team.
- Wade plays on the soccer team.
- Young plays on the football team plus at least one other team.
- No team includes both Wade and Zuckerman.

19. If Wade plays on the football team and Young doesn't play on the soccer team, which of the following is a complete listing of the number of these four students who must be on each team?

(A) baseball: 2; football: 2; soccer: 2
(B) baseball: 2; football: 3; soccer: 2
(C) baseball: 2; football: 3; soccer: 3
(D) baseball: 3; football: 2; soccer: 3
(E) baseball: 3; football: 3; soccer: 2

20. If Wade plays on the football team, which of the following is a complete list of the students who could play on the soccer team?

(A) Vickery, Wade
(B) Wade, Young
(C) Vickery, Wade, Young
(D) Vickery, Young, Zuckerman
(E) Vickery, Wade, Young, Zuckerman

21. If only one of these four students plays on the baseball team, which of the following statements must be true?

(A) One of these students plays on the football team and three play on the soccer team.

(B) Two of these students play on the football team and two play on the soccer team.

(C) Two of these students play on the football team and three play on the soccer team.

(D) Three of these students play on the football team and two play on the soccer team.

(E) Three of these students play on the football team and three play on the soccer team.

22. If Young doesn't play on the soccer team, which of the following pairs of students must play on the football team?

(A) Vickery and Wade

(B) Vickery and Young

(C) Vickery and Zuckerman

(D) Wade and Young

(E) Young and Zuckerman

23. If Zuckerman doesn't play on the baseball team, which of the following statements CANNOT be true?

(A) Vickery plays on both the baseball team and the football team.

(B) Vickery plays on both the baseball team and the soccer team.

(C) Wade plays on both the baseball team and the soccer team.

(D) Wade plays on both the football team and the soccer team.

(E) Young plays on both the football team and the soccer team.

STOP

If you finish before time is up, you may check your work.
Solutions are on pages 114–115.

LOGIC GAME 1

Six people—F, G, H, K, L, and M—have birthdays during six consecutive months, from July to December. No two people have birthdays during the same month.

- Either F or M has a birthday in September.
- G and H have birthdays that are two months apart, in some order.
- L has a birthday in either August or October.
- If K's birthday is in July, then M's birthday is in November; otherwise, G's birthday is not in October.

1. Which of the following could be the order, from July to December, in which the six people have birthdays?

(A) F, M, L, G, K, H
(B) K, L, F, M, G, H
(C) K, L, M, H, F, G
(D) L, M, F, H, K, G
(E) M, L, F, H, K, G

2. Which of the following must be true?

(A) F's birthday is in September.
(B) G's birthday is in December.
(C) H's birthday is in October.
(D) L's birthday is in August.
(E) M's birthday is in November.

3. Which of the following is a complete list of the months in which M could have been born?

(A) July and September
(B) July and November
(C) September and November
(D) July, September, and November
(E) July, September, November, and December

4. If K was born in July, which of the following CANNOT be true?

    (A) F was born in September.
    (B) G was born in October.
    (C) H was born in December.
    (D) L was born in August.
    (E) M was born in September.

5. If G's birthday is not in October, which of the following is a complete list of the people whose birthday could be in July?

    (A) F and K
    (B) F and M
    (C) F, K, and M
    (D) F, G, K, and M
    (E) F, G, H, K, and M

GO ON TO THE NEXT PAGE

LOGIC GAME 2

At least two cars were selected for use from a set of six cars—an Audi, a BMW, a Ford, a Kia, a Toyota, and a Volvo—according to the following restrictions:

- The Audi was selected if and only if the Ford was not selected.
- If the Kia was selected, then the Toyota was not selected.
- If the Toyota was selected, then the Volvo was not selected.
- If the Volvo was selected, then neither the Audi nor the BMW was selected.

6. Which of the following could be a complete listing of the cars that were and were not selected?

   (A) selected: Audi, BMW, Kia, Volvo
       not selected: Ford, Toyota
   (B) selected: Audi, Ford
       not selected: BMW, Kia, Toyota, Volvo
   (C) selected: Audi, Kia, Toyota
       not selected: BMW, Ford, Volvo
   (D) selected: Ford, Toyota, Volvo
       not selected: Audi, BMW, Kia
   (E) selected: Ford, Kia
       not selected: Audi, BMW, Toyota, Volvo

7. If the BMW was selected, which of the following CANNOT have been selected?

   (A) the Audi
   (B) the Ford
   (C) the Kia
   (D) the Toyota
   (E) the Volvo

8. If the Volvo was selected, then which of the other cars must also have been selected?

   (A) the Audi
   (B) the BMW
   (C) the Ford
   (D) the Kia
   (E) the Toyota

9. Which of the following pairs of cars could have been selected?

(A) the Audi and the Ford
(B) the BMW and the Volvo
(C) the Ford and the Kia
(D) the Kia and the Toyota
(E) the Toyota and the Volvo

10. If the Toyota was selected, which of the following is a complete list of the cars that also could have been selected?

(A) Ford, Kia
(B) Audi, BMW, Ford
(C) Audi, BMW
(D) Audi, Ford, Kia
(E) Audi, BMW, Ford, Kia

11. What is the maximum number of cars that could have been selected?

(A) 2
(B) 3
(C) 4
(D) 5
(E) 6

GO ON TO THE NEXT PAGE

LOGIC GAME 3

Six friends surnamed Taylor, Underwood, Vasquez, Walker, Yeager, and Zaines are sitting around a circular table. The following conditions hold:

- Taylor is sitting next to Yeager.
- Vasquez is immediately to the left of Zaines.
- Underwood and Yeager aren't sitting next to each other.
- Walker and Zaines aren't sitting next to each other.

12. Which of the following could be a complete list of the six friends in clockwise order around the table?

    (A) Taylor, Yeager, Walker, Vasquez, Zaines, Underwood
    (B) Underwood, Zaines, Vasquez, Yeager, Walker, Taylor
    (C) Vasquez, Yeager, Taylor, Walker, Underwood, Zaines
    (D) Walker, Zaines, Vasquez, Yeager, Taylor, Underwood
    (E) Zaines, Vasquez, Walker, Underwood, Yeager, Taylor

13. If Taylor is sitting next to Zaines, which of the following pairs of people must be sitting next to each other?

    (A) Taylor and Underwood
    (B) Underwood and Zaines
    (C) Walker and Yeager
    (D) Vasquez and Walker
    (E) Yeager and Zaines

14. If Yeager and Vasquez are sitting next to each other, which of the following pairs of friends must both be sitting next to Underwood?

    (A) Taylor and Vasquez
    (B) Taylor and Walker
    (C) Taylor and Zaines
    (D) Vasquez and Walker
    (E) Walker and Zaines

15. If Yeager is sitting next to Zaines, which of the following is a complete list of the people who could be sitting next to Walker?

(A) Taylor, Underwood, Vasquez
(B) Taylor, Underwood, Yeager
(C) Taylor, Vasquez, Yeager
(D) Underwood, Vasquez, Yeager
(E) Taylor, Underwood, Vasquez, Yeager

16. If Vasquez and Walker are sitting next to each other, which of the following is a complete list of the people who must be sitting next to Underwood?

(A) Taylor
(B) Walker
(C) Zaines
(D) Taylor and Walker
(E) Taylor and Zaines

17. If Walker and Yeager aren't sitting next to each other, all of the following pairs of friends could be sitting next to each other EXCEPT:

(A) Taylor and Underwood
(B) Taylor and Zaines
(C) Underwood and Vasquez
(D) Vasquez and Walker
(E) Vasquez and Yeager

GO ON TO THE NEXT PAGE

LOGIC GAME 4

A television station will fill the 8 P.M.–11 P.M. time slot with four half-hour shows—N, O, P, and Q—and one one-hour show—M. The following guidelines will be observed:

- The one-hour show will start airing at 8:00, 9:00, or 10:00.
- N will air sometime after P and sometime before Q.
- O will air either immediately before or immediately after Q.

18. Which of the following could be a complete listing of the five shows in the order in which they will air?

   (A) M, N, P, O, Q
   (B) M, P, O, Q, N
   (C) O, P, M, N, Q
   (D) P, M, N, Q, O
   (E) P, N, O, Q, M

19. Which of the following is a complete list of the shows that could air at 9:00?

   (A) M, P
   (B) M, O, Q
   (C) M, N, P
   (D) M, O, P, Q
   (E) M, N, O, P, Q

20. Which of the following is a complete list of the shows that could start airing at 9:30?

   (A) N, O, Q
   (B) N, P, Q
   (C) O, P, Q
   (D) M, N, O, Q
   (E) N, O, P, Q

21. Which of the following is a complete list of the times at which N could air?

   (A) 8:30 and 9:00
   (B) 8:30 and 9:30
   (C) 9:00 and 9:30
   (D) 8:30, 9:00, and 9:30
   (E) 8:30, 9:00, 9:30, and 10:00

22. If O airs at 10:00, which of the following statements could be true?

   (A) M airs at 8:00 and P airs at 9:30.
   (B) M airs at 8:00 and Q airs at 9:30.
   (C) N airs at 8:00 and M airs at 9:00.
   (D) P airs at 8:00 and M airs at 9:00.
   (E) P airs at 8:30 and M airs at 9:00.

23. If M airs either immediately before or immediately after Q, which of the following statements must be FALSE?

   (A) M airs immediately before P.
   (B) N airs immediately before M.
   (C) N airs immediately before O.
   (D) O airs immediately before Q.
   (E) Q airs immediately before O.

STOP

If you finish before time is up, you may check your work.
Solutions are on pages 116–117.

LOGIC GAME 1

Six people—U, V, W, X, Y, and Z—checked into a hotel the same week, from Monday to Saturday, with no two checking in the same day.

- U checked in sometime after Y but sometime before Z.
- X checked in sometime after both V and Z.
- W checked in either Monday or Saturday.

1. Which of the following could be the order in which the six people checked in?

   (A) V, Y, U, Z, W, X
   (B) W, U, Y, V, Z, X
   (C) W, Y, V, U, Z, X
   (D) Y, U, Z, X, V, W
   (E) Y, V, Z, U, X, W

2. A complete list of the people who could have checked in on Monday is:

   (A) Y
   (B) V and W
   (C) V and Y
   (D) W and Y
   (E) V, W, and Y

3. If V checked in on Monday, which of the following must have checked in on Thursday?

   (A) U
   (B) W
   (C) X
   (D) Y
   (E) Z

4. If Z checked in on Friday, which of the following is a complete list of the days on which Y could have checked in?

(A) Tuesday and Wednesday
(B) Wednesday and Thursday
(C) Tuesday, Wednesday, and Thursday
(D) Monday, Tuesday, and Wednesday
(E) Monday, Tuesday, Wednesday, and Thursday

5. If X checked in on Friday, which of the following statements must be true?

(A) Y checked in on Monday.
(B) U checked in on Tuesday.
(C) U checked in on Wednesday.
(D) Z checked in on Thursday.
(E) W checked in on Saturday.

6. V could have checked in the day before any person EXCEPT:

(A) U
(B) W
(C) X
(D) Y
(E) Z

GO ON TO THE NEXT PAGE

LOGIC GAME 2

Members of a tennis team are being considered for a mixed-doubles exhibition, which will include two women and two men. The team includes four women—Irene, Jasmine, Kate, and Louisa—and four men—Pete, Roger, Sven, and Tomas. The following conditions hold:

- If Jasmine is included, then neither Louisa nor Pete will be included.
- If Kate is included, then Irene will not be included but Roger will be.
- If Sven is not included, then Irene and Tomas will both be included.

7. If neither Kate nor Louisa is included, which of the following is a complete list of the men who could be included?

    (A) Pete, Roger
    (B) Roger, Sven
    (C) Roger, Tomas
    (D) Sven, Tomas
    (E) Roger, Sven, Tomas

8. If Jasmine and Tomas are both included, all of the following could be true EXCEPT:

    (A) Irene is included.
    (B) Kate is included.
    (C) Pete is not included.
    (D) Roger is not included.
    (E) Sven is included.

9. If Kate is included, which of the following could be true?

    (A) Irene is included and Pete is not included.
    (B) Jasmine is included and Roger is not included.
    (C) Jasmine is not included and Sven is not included.
    (D) Louisa is not included and Pete is included.
    (E) Louisa is included and Tomas is not included.

10. If Sven is not included, all of the following pairs could both be included EXCEPT:

(A) Jasmine and Pete
(B) Jasmine and Roger
(C) Louisa and Pete
(D) Louisa and Roger
(E) Louisa and Tomas

11. If Pete is included but Roger is not included, which of the following statements must be true?

(A) Either Irene or Louisa is included, but not both of them.
(B) Either Irene or Sven is included, but not both of them.
(C) Either Sven or Tomas is included, but not both of them.
(D) Either Kate or Sven is included, but not both of them.
(E) Either Louisa or Tomas is included, but not both of them.

12. If both Irene and Roger are included, which of the following is a complete list of the people who CANNOT be included?

(A) Kate
(B) Pete
(C) Sven
(D) Kate and Sven
(E) Kate and Pete

GO ON TO THE NEXT PAGE

LOGIC GAME 3

On five consecutive days, Edith played cards with five different friends (Ms. Minsky, Ms. Norris, Ms. Olsen, Mr. Smith, and Mr. Truong). Each day, she played either gin rummy or pinochle exclusively, though over the course of the five days she played each game at least once. The following restrictions apply:

- She played pinochle on the first day with a woman.
- She played gin rummy with Ms. Olsen.
- Mr. Smith was the first of the two men with whom Edith played cards.
- She never played gin rummy on two consecutive days.

13. Which of the following could be a complete listing, in order, of the five people with whom Edith played cards?

(A) Ms. Minsky, Mr. Smith, Ms. Olsen, Mr. Truong, Ms. Norris
(B) Ms. Minsky, Mr. Truong, Mr. Smith, Ms. Norris, Ms. Olsen
(C) Ms. Norris, Ms. Olsen, Mr. Truong, Mr. Smith, Ms. Minsky
(D) Ms. Olsen, Ms. Norris, Ms. Minsky, Mr. Smith, Mr. Truong
(E) Mr. Smith, Mr. Truong, Ms. Olsen, Ms. Minsky, Ms. Norris

14. If Edith played gin rummy with Ms. Norris on the third day, which of the following statements must be true?

(A) She played Ms. Minsky the day before she played Ms. Norris.
(B) She played Ms. Minsky the day before she played Mr. Smith.
(C) She played Ms. Norris the day before she played Mr. Smith.
(D) She played Ms. Olsen the day before she played Mr. Truong.
(E) She played Mr. Smith the day before she played Mr. Truong.

15. If Edith played cards with Ms. Olsen the day before she played cards with Ms. Minsky, then each of the following statements could be true EXCEPT:

(A) On the second day, she played gin rummy with Mr. Smith.
(B) On the second day, she played pinochle with Mr. Smith.
(C) On the third day, she played pinochle with Mr. Smith.
(D) On the fourth day, she played pinochle with Ms. Minsky.
(E) On the fifth day, she played gin rummy with Mr. Truong.

16. If Edith had played cards with Ms. Olsen, Mr. Smith, and Ms. Norris in order, though not necessarily consecutively, then which of the following statements must be true?

(A) She played gin rummy with Ms. Minsky.
(B) She played gin rummy with Ms. Norris.
(C) She played pinochle with Ms. Norris.
(D) She played pinochle with Mr. Smith.
(E) She played pinochle with Mr. Truong.

17. If Edith played gin rummy with Mr. Smith, which of the following statements CANNOT be true?

(A) She played Ms. Minsky two days before she played Ms. Olsen.
(B) She played Ms. Norris three days before she played Ms. Olsen.
(C) She played Ms. Olsen the day before she played Mr. Truong.
(D) She played Ms. Olsen two days before she played Mr. Truong.
(E) She played Ms. Olsen three days before she played Mr. Truong.

18. If on the third and fourth days, Edith played two different games with Ms. Norris and Mr. Truong, respectively, which of the following statements could be true?

(A) She played gin rummy with Ms. Minsky and pinochle with Mr. Smith.
(B) She played pinochle with Ms. Minsky and gin rummy with Mr. Truong.
(C) She played gin rummy with Ms. Norris and pinochle with Mr. Smith.
(D) She played gin rummy with Mr. Smith and pinochle with Mr. Truong.
(E) She played pinochle with Mr. Smith and gin rummy with Mr. Truong.

GO ON TO THE NEXT PAGE

LOGIC GAME 4

A game uses a pack of 20 cards, numbered from 1 to 20. Players may play cards in accordance with the following rules:

- Once a card has been played, no player during that round may play a lower card.
- When an even-numbered card is played, the next card must be odd.
- When an odd-numbered card is played, the next card must be at least 3 greater than that card.
- When a card is played of value 18, 19, or 20, the round is over.

19. Which of the following could be a complete list of all the cards played in a single round, in order?

(A) 2, 7, 9, 13, 14, 19
(B) 4, 11, 15, 16, 18
(C) 5, 10, 9, 12, 15, 20
(D) 6, 9, 12, 13, 19
(E) 7, 10, 15, 18, 19

20. If only odd-numbered cards are played in a round, what is the maximum number of cards that could be played in that round?

(A) 5
(B) 6
(C) 7
(D) 8
(E) 9

21. If the second card played in a round is a 6, which of the following cards could have been the first card played?

(A) 2
(B) 3
(C) 4
(D) 5
(E) 7

22. If the fourth card in a round is a 10, a complete list of the cards that could have been played second in that round is:

(A) 3, 4
(B) 4, 5
(C) 3, 4, 6
(D) 2, 3, 4, 5
(E) 2, 3, 4, 6

23. If the rule stating that when an odd-numbered card is played, the next card must be at least 3 greater than that card, is changed to state that when an odd-numbered card is played, the next card must be at least 6 greater than that card, how many different cards CANNOT be played as the second card in a round?

(A) 1
(B) 2
(C) 3
(D) 4
(E) 5

STOP

If you finish before time is up, you may check your work.
Solutions are on pages 118–119.

LOGIC GAME 1

The eight members of the conference committee for a club—S, T, U, V, W, X, Y, and Z—voted to decide whether to hold their yearly conference in Houston or Indianapolis. Four members voted for each location according to the following conditions:

- Either S or V, or both, voted to hold the conference in Houston.
- T and U voted to hold the conference in different cities.
- If W voted to hold the conference in Indianapolis, then so did X.
- If Y voted to hold the conference in Houston, then V voted to hold it in Indianapolis.

1. Which of the following could be a complete listing of the votes cast for the two cities?

   (A) Houston: S, T, U, Z; Indianapolis: V, W, X, Y
   (B) Houston: T, V, X, Z; Indianapolis: S, U, W, Y
   (C) Houston: T, W, Y, Z; Indianapolis: S, U, V, X
   (D) Houston: U, V, W, Y; Indianapolis: S, T, X, Z
   (E) Houston: U, V, W, Z; Indianapolis: S, T, X, Y

2. Which of the following pairs of committee members could NOT both have voted to hold the conference in Houston?

   (A) S and Y
   (B) T and X
   (C) W and X
   (D) X and Z
   (E) Y and Z

3. If S voted to hold the conference in Indianapolis, which of the following pairs must both have voted to hold the conference in the same city?

   (A) V and W
   (B) V and X
   (C) V and Z
   (D) W and X
   (E) W and Z

4. If X voted to hold the conference in Houston, which of the following must have voted to hold the conference in Indianapolis?

(A) S
(B) U
(C) V
(D) W
(E) Y

5. If both U and Y voted to hold the conference in Houston, which of the following is a complete list of the committee members who could have voted to hold it in Indianapolis?

(A) T, V, W, X
(B) T, V, X, Z
(C) S, T, W, X, Z
(D) T, V, W, X, Z
(E) S, T, V, W, X, Z

6. If W and Y both voted to hold the conference in the same city, which of the following statements must be true?

(A) S voted to hold the conference in Indianapolis.
(B) V voted to hold the conference in Houston.
(C) V voted to hold the conference in Indianapolis.
(D) X voted to hold the conference in Indianapolis.
(E) Z voted to hold the conference in Houston.

7. Which of the following lists of four committee members could have voted as a group to hold the conference in Houston, and could also have voted as a group to hold the conference in Indianapolis?

(A) S, T, V, and W
(B) S, T, Y, and Z
(C) S, U, V, and Z
(D) S, U, W, and Z
(E) U, V, X, and Z

GO ON TO THE NEXT PAGE

LOGIC GAME 2

A school trip to a museum included eight children—four girls named Holly, Jenn, Marta, and Olivia, and four boys named Raoul, Trevor, Will, and Xavier. All of the children viewed the Egyptian exhibit in pairs who entered the exhibit at 1:00, 1:20, 1:40, and 2:00, according to the following conditions:

- Two girls entered the exhibit at 1:20.
- Trevor entered the exhibit at an earlier time than Olivia.
- Marta and Will entered the exhibit together.
- Xavier didn't enter the exhibit at 1:00.

8. If Raoul entered the exhibit at 1:40, which of the following statements could be true?

   (A) Holly entered at 2:00.
   (B) Jenn entered at 1:40.
   (C) Olivia entered at 1:40.
   (D) Trevor entered at 1:40.
   (E) Xavier entered at 1:00.

9. If Xavier didn't enter the exhibit at 1:40, which of the following is a complete list of the children who could have entered the exhibit at the same time as Xavier?

   (A) Holly, Jenn
   (B) Holly, Jenn, Olivia
   (C) Holly, Jenn, Olivia, Raoul
   (D) Holly, Jenn, Olivia, Trevor
   (E) Holly, Jenn, Olivia, Raoul, Trevor

10. If Olivia and Xavier entered the exhibit together, which of the following is a complete list of the times at which Jenn could have entered the exhibit?

    (A) 1:20
    (B) 1:00, 1:20
    (C) 1:20, 1:40
    (D) 1:00, 1:20, 1:40
    (E) 1:00, 1:20, 1:40, 2:00

11. If Olivia entered the exhibit 20 minutes before Raoul, which of the following statements must be true?

(A) Holly entered at 1:00.
(B) Jenn entered at 1:20.
(C) Marta entered at 1:40.
(D) Trevor entered at 1:00.
(E) Xavier entered at 2:00.

12. Each of the following children could have entered the exhibit with Holly EXCEPT:

(A) Jenn
(B) Olivia
(C) Raoul
(D) Trevor
(E) Xavier

GO ON TO THE NEXT PAGE

LOGIC GAME 3

On seven different days last month (from the 1st to the 7th) Elizabeth had appointments in different cities: F, G, H, J, K, M, N, and P. She visited at least one city each day, and visited two different cities on one of the days, according to the following restrictions.

- Elizabeth visited only one city on the 5th.
- She visited F, H, and J on three consecutive days, in that order.
- She visited N two days before she visited P and two days after she visited M.
- She visited G sometime before she visited K.

13. If Elizabeth visited only J on the 3rd, which city must she have visited on the 5th?

(A) G
(B) K
(C) M
(D) N
(E) P

14. If Elizabeth visited K on the 6th, which city must she have visited on the 5th?

(A) G
(B) H
(C) J
(D) N
(E) P

15. If Elizabeth visited two cities on the 2nd, which city must she have visited on the 4th?

(A) F
(B) G
(C) H
(D) K
(E) N

16. If Elizabeth visited F on the first day, which of the following is a complete listing of the days on which she could have visited P?

(A) 6th
(B) 7th
(C) 5th, 6th
(D) 6th, 7th
(E) 5th, 6th, 7th

17. If Elizabeth visited P and one other city on the same day, which city must she have visited on the day before that?

(A) F
(B) G
(C) H
(D) J
(E) K

18. Elizabeth could have visited each of the following pairs of cities on the same day EXCEPT:

(A) H and M
(B) H and N
(C) H and P
(D) J and M
(E) J and P

GO ON TO THE NEXT PAGE

LOGIC GAME 4

A play has five performances per week: one on Friday evening, two on Saturday (afternoon and evening), and two on Sunday (afternoon and evening). The lead male role is played by two different actors—Mr. Wicks and Mr. Yeats—each of whom appears in at least one performance. The lead female role is played by three different actresses—Ms. Quinn, Ms. Rosen, and Ms. Stein—each of whom appears in at least one performance. The following restrictions apply:

- All of Mr. Wicks's performances occur before all of Mr. Yeats's.
- No actress appears in two performances on the same day.
- Ms. Quinn does not appear on Saturday.
- Ms. Rosen and Mr. Yeats never appear together in the same performance.

19. If Ms. Rosen has exactly two performances per week and no actress appears in any two consecutive performances, all of the following statements could be true EXCEPT:

(A) Ms. Quinn has two evening performances.
(B) Ms. Rosen has two afternoon performances.
(C) Ms. Stein has two afternoon performances.
(D) Mr. Wicks has two evening performances.
(E) Mr. Yeats has two evening performances.

20. If Ms. Quinn doesn't appear on Sunday, which of the following pairs of actors must appear in the same number of performances per week?

(A) Ms. Quinn and Mr. Wicks
(B) Ms. Quinn and Mr. Yeats
(C) Ms. Rosen and Mr. Wicks
(D) Ms. Rosen and Mr. Yeats
(E) Ms. Stein and Mr. Wicks

21. If no actor-actress pair appears together in more than one performance per week, which of the following statements must be true?

(A) Ms. Quinn appears on Friday evening and Mr. Yeats appears on Sunday afternoon.

(B) Ms. Quinn appears on Sunday evening and Mr. Wicks appears on Sunday afternoon.

(C) Ms. Rosen appears on Saturday afternoon and Mr. Yeats appears on Sunday afternoon.

(D) Ms. Stein appears on Saturday evening and Mr. Yeats appears on Sunday evening.

(E) Ms. Stein appears on Sunday evening and Mr. Yeats appears on Sunday afternoon.

22. If Ms. Stein only performs with Mr. Yeats, which of the following statements must be true?

(A) Ms. Rosen appears in exactly two performances.

(B) Ms. Quinn appears in exactly two performances.

(C) Mr. Wicks appears in exactly three performances.

(D) Mr. Yeats appears in exactly three performances.

(E) Mr. Wicks appears in exactly four performances.

23. If the Saturday evening and Sunday afternoon performances feature the same lead actor and actress, which of the following performers CANNOT appear in exactly two performances per week?

(A) Ms. Quinn

(B) Ms. Rosen

(C) Ms. Stein

(D) Mr. Wicks

(E) Mr. Yeats

STOP

If you finish before time is up, you may check your work.
Solutions are on pages 120–121.

LOGIC GAME 1

A horror film festival featured eight films on eight consecutive days. Each film was about either vampires, werewolves, or zombies, according to the following conditions:

- No two films on two consecutive days were about the same type of monster.
- The first and last films were either both about werewolves or both about zombies.
- Either the third film was about vampires and the sixth film was about zombies, or the third film was about zombies and the sixth was about werewolves.
- Either the fourth or the fifth film was about vampires.

1. Which of the following could be a complete list of the monsters featured, in order, in each of the eight films?

   (A) werewolves, zombies, vampires, zombies, werewolves, zombies, vampires, werewolves
   (B) werewolves, vampires, zombies, vampires, zombies, werewolves, zombies, werewolves
   (C) werewolves, zombies, vampires, werewolves, vampires, zombies, werewolves, zombies
   (D) zombies, vampires, zombies, werewolves, vampires, werewolves, werewolves, zombies
   (E) zombies, werewolves, vampires, zombies, vampires, werewolves, vampires, zombies

2. If movies about zombies were shown on the first, third, and fifth days, what would be the greatest number of films that could feature vampires?

   (A) 0
   (B) 1
   (C) 2
   (D) 3
   (E) 4

3. If the first three movies featured werewolves, vampires, and zombies, in that order, which of the following statements must be FALSE?

(A) The fourth movie featured vampires.
(B) The fourth movie featured werewolves.
(C) The fifth movie featured vampires.
(D) The fifth movie featured werewolves.
(E) The fifth movie featured zombies.

4. If the last movie about vampires was shown on the fourth day, what is the minimum number of movies about zombies that could have been shown?

(A) 0
(B) 1
(C) 2
(D) 3
(E) 4

5. What is the last possible day on which the first movie about werewolves could have been shown?

(A) second
(B) third
(C) fourth
(D) fifth
(E) sixth

GO ON TO THE NEXT PAGE

LOGIC GAME 2

Six people—N, O, P, Q, R, and S—were each interviewed for a job individually, with no two being interviewed at the same time, according to the following constraints:

- Either O or S was interviewed third.
- Q was interviewed sometime before R and sometime after P.
- If N was interviewed second, then S was interviewed fifth; otherwise, O was interviewed second.

6. Which of the following could be the order in which the six people were interviewed?

   (A) N, O, S, P, Q, R
   (B) N, P, O, S, Q, R
   (C) P, N, O, R, S, Q
   (D) P, N, S, Q, O, R
   (E) S, O, P, N, Q, R

7. If N was interviewed fourth, which of the following must have been interviewed fifth?

   (A) O
   (B) P
   (C) Q
   (D) R
   (E) S

8. If N was interviewed fifth, which of the following must have been interviewed immediately after S?

   (A) N
   (B) O
   (C) P
   (D) Q
   (E) R

9. If Q was interviewed fourth, which of the following is a complete list of the people who could have been interviewed fifth?

(A) N and O
(B) N and R
(C) O and R
(D) N, R, and S
(E) O, R, and S

10. If the third and fourth people to be interviewed were both called back for a second interview, and one of them was subsequently hired, which of the interviewees could NOT have been hired?

(A) N
(B) O
(C) P
(D) R
(E) S

11. If the fourth and fifth people to be interviewed were both called back for a second interview, and BOTH of them were subsequently hired, which of the interviewees must have been hired?

(A) N
(B) P
(C) Q
(D) R
(E) S

GO ON TO THE NEXT PAGE

LOGIC GAME 3

On five consecutive days, Lauren worked for five different clients: F, G, H, J, and K. For each client, she did either Palette Deco, stencil, or Venetian plaster.

- On the second day, she did a stencil.
- On the fourth day, she worked for F.
- On the fifth day, she did Palette Deco.
- She did Venetian plaster for G sometime before she worked for J.

12. Which of the following could be a list of Lauren's five clients in the order in which she worked for them?

    (A) G, J, F, H, K
    (B) K, G, J, F, H
    (C) H, J, G, F, K
    (D) H, K, G, F, J
    (E) K, G, H, F, J

13. If Lauren's first client was K, which of the following statements must be true?

    (A) She did Venetian plaster for F.
    (B) She did Palette Deco for F.
    (C) She did Palette Deco for H.
    (D) She did a stencil for H.
    (E) She did Venetian plaster for J.

14. If Lauren did Venetian plaster for H, each of the following statements could be true EXCEPT:

    (A) She did G's job first.
    (B) She did G's job third.
    (C) She did J's job second.
    (D) She did J's job third.
    (E) She did K's job fifth.

15. If Lauren did G's job the day before she did K's job, for which of the following pairs of customers must she have worked on consecutive days, in either order?

(A) F and G
(B) F and J
(C) G and J
(D) H and J
(E) H and K

16. If Lauren worked for H and J on consecutive days, in some order, which of the following statements must be true?

(A) She did Venetian plaster for F.
(B) She did a stencil for H.
(C) She did Palette Deco for J.
(D) She did a stencil for J.
(E) She did Palette Deco for K.

17. If Lauren did the same type of finish for J and K, which of the following is a complete list of the people for whom she could have done Venetian plaster?

(A) G
(B) F and G
(C) G and H
(D) G, J, and K
(E) F, G, and H

18. If Lauren's only two Venetian plaster jobs were third and fourth, which of the following statements must be true?

(A) She did Palette Deco for either F or H.
(B) She did a stencil for either F or J.
(C) She did a stencil for either F or K.
(D) She did a stencil for either H or K.
(E) She did Venetian plaster for either H or K.

GO ON TO THE NEXT PAGE

LOGIC GAME 4

In a single one-week period, Danielle went running on four different days, in each case in one of four locations—up a hill, in a park, around a reservoir, or on a track.

- She ran up a hill either two days before or two days after she ran around a reservoir.
- She ran in a park either three days before or three days after she ran on a track.
- She ran around a reservoir either four days before or four days after she ran on a track.

19. If Danielle went running on the sixth day, on which day must she NOT have gone running?

(A) first
(B) second
(C) third
(D) fourth
(E) fifth

20. If Danielle ran up a hill on the first day, which of the following is a complete list of the days when she must NOT have gone running?

(A) second, third, fifth
(B) second, third, sixth
(C) second, fifth, sixth
(D) third, fourth, sixth
(E) third, fifth, sixth

21. If Danielle didn't run on the third day, which of the following is a complete list of the days on which she could have run around a reservoir?

(A) fifth
(B) sixth
(C) seventh
(D) fifth, sixth
(E) sixth, seventh

22. If Danielle ran on the track on the fifth day, which of the following statements must be FALSE?

(A) On the first day she ran around a reservoir.
(B) On the second day she ran in a park.
(C) On the fourth day she ran up a hill.
(D) On the sixth day she didn't run.
(E) On the seventh day she didn't run.

23. If Danielle ran in a park on the fourth day, which of the following is a complete list of the places she could have run on the fifth day?

(A) up a hill
(B) around a reservoir
(C) up a hill, around a reservoir
(D) up a hill, on a track
(E) up a hill, around a reservoir, on a track

STOP

If you finish before time is up, you may check your work.
Solutions are on pages 122–123.

LOGIC GAME 1

Six employees—Fran, Gloria, Hank, Ivan, Jessica, and Keith—are being considered for a special training program. At least one of the group is selected and at least one is not selected, according to the following constraints:

- If Hank is selected, then Gloria is also selected.
- If Gloria is selected, then Ivan is not selected.
- If Ivan is selected, then Jessica is not selected.
- If Keith is selected, then Jessica is also selected.

1. Which of the following pairs of employees could be the only two employees who are selected?

    (A) Fran and Hank
    (B) Fran and Jessica
    (C) Gloria and Ivan
    (D) Hank and Jessica
    (E) Hank and Keith

2. Which employee could be the only employee NOT selected?

    (A) Fran
    (B) Hank
    (C) Ivan
    (D) Jessica
    (E) Keith

3. If Keith is selected and exactly two other employees are selected, each of the following statements could be true EXCEPT:

    (A) Fran is selected.
    (B) Fran is not selected.
    (C) Gloria is selected.
    (D) Gloria is not selected.
    (E) Hank is selected.

4. If Gloria and exactly one other employee are selected, which of the following statements could be true?

(A) Hank is selected.
(B) Ivan is selected.
(C) Ivan is selected.
(D) Keith is selected.
(E) Fran, Hank, and Jessica are all not selected.

5. Which of the following is a complete list of the employees that could be the only employee selected?

(A) Fran
(B) Fran, Gloria
(C) Fran, Gloria, Ivan
(D) Fran, Gloria, Jessica
(E) Fran, Gloria, Ivan, Jessica

GO ON TO THE NEXT PAGE

LOGIC GAME 2

Nine people (F, G, H, J, K, L, M, N, and P) are standing in a line:

- L is someplace in front of M but someplace behind P.
- K is behind both F and M.
- G is at least two places behind K.
- F and H are standing next to each other, in some order.

6. Which of the following is a complete list of the people who could be first in line?

(A) J and N
(B) J, N, and P
(C) F, J, N, and P
(D) H, J, N, and P
(E) F, H, J, N, and P

7. L could be standing in any of the following positions EXCEPT:

(A) second
(B) third
(C) fourth
(D) fifth
(E) sixth

8. If N is standing directly in front of J, which of the following people CANNOT be third in line?

(A) F
(B) H
(C) L
(D) M
(E) P

9. If M is third in line, which of the following is a complete list of the people who could be fifth in line?

(A) F and H
(B) J and N
(C) F, H, and K
(D) J, K, and N
(E) F, H, J, K, and N

10. If K is not sixth in line, then J could be standing next to each of the following people EXCEPT:

(A) K
(B) L
(C) M
(D) N
(E) P

11. Which of the following is a complete list of the people who could be last in line?

(A) J
(B) N
(C) J and N
(D) G, J, and N
(E) G, H, J, and N

GO ON TO THE NEXT PAGE

LOGIC GAME 3

A card game includes cards of five colors—blue, green, orange, red, and yellow. A game proceeds with the following rules:

- The first player can play either a blue card or a green card.
- If a player plays a blue card, the next player must play either a green card or a yellow card.
- If a player plays a green card, the next player must play either an orange card or a yellow card
- If a player plays an orange card, the next player must play either a blue card or a red card.
- If a player plays a red card, the next player must play a blue card.
- The round ends when either a yellow card is played or 8 cards have been played, whichever comes first.

12. Which of the following could be a complete list, in order, of all the cards played in a single round of the game?

    (A) blue, green, red, blue, green, yellow
    (B) green, orange, red, blue, green, yellow, red
    (C) blue, green, orange, blue, green, orange, red, blue
    (D) green, orange, red, blue, green, blue, orange, yellow
    (E) blue, green, orange, red, blue, green, orange, blue, yellow

13. Which of the following is a complete list of the colors that could be played third?

    (A) blue, green, orange, red
    (B) blue, green, orange, yellow
    (C) blue, orange, red, yellow
    (D) green, orange, red, yellow
    (E) blue, green, orange, red, yellow

14. If the first card played in a round is blue, then which of the following is a complete list of the cards that could be played fifth?

    (A) blue, green, yellow
    (B) blue, green, orange, yellow
    (C) blue, green, orange, red
    (D) blue, green, red, yellow
    (E) blue, green, orange, red, yellow

15. If the second and fifth cards played in a round are both orange, then the fourth card must be which of the following colors?

(A) blue
(B) green
(C) orange
(D) red
(E) yellow

16. If the fourth card played in a round is blue, then the second card played in that round could have been which of the following?

(A) blue or green
(B) blue or orange
(C) blue or red
(D) green or orange
(E) orange or red

17. If the sixth card played in a round is red, then the second card played in that round must have been which of the following?

(A) blue
(B) green
(C) orange
(D) red
(E) yellow

18. Which of the following is the maximum number of green cards that could be played in a single round?

(A) 1
(B) 2
(C) 3
(D) 4
(E) 5

GO ON TO THE NEXT PAGE

LOGIC GAME 4

Six people—Tom, Ursula, Victor, Wendy, Xavier, and Yolanda—are sitting at a round table eating ice cream. Each is eating one of four different flavors of ice cream—orange sorbet, pistachio, rocky road, and strawberry—and at least one person is eating each flavor. A list of the six people, in clockwise order around the table, is as follows:

- Tom
- a person who is eating rocky road
- Wendy
- Xavier
- a person who is eating strawberry
- the only person who is eating orange sorbet

19. Which of the following is a complete list of the flavors that Tom could be eating?

   (A) pistachio
   (B) rocky road, strawberry
   (C) orange sorbet, rocky road, strawberry
   (D) pistachio, rocky road, strawberry
   (E) orange sorbet, pistachio, rocky road, strawberry

20. Which of the following is a complete list of the flavors that Ursula could be eating?

   (A) orange sorbet, pistachio, rocky road
   (B) orange sorbet, pistachio, strawberry
   (C) orange sorbet, rocky road, strawberry
   (D) pistachio, rocky road, strawberry
   (E) orange sorbet, pistachio, rocky road, strawberry

21. If Ursula and Victor are sitting next to each other, which of the following is a complete list of the flavors of ice cream that Yolanda could be eating?

   (A) pistachio
   (B) rocky road
   (C) pistachio, rocky road
   (D) pistachio, rocky road, strawberry
   (E) orange sorbet, pistachio, rocky road, strawberry

22. If three people are eating the same flavor of ice cream and no two of these people are sitting next to each other, which of the following statements must be true?

(A) Tom is eating pistachio.
(B) Tom is eating rocky road.
(C) Wendy is eating rocky road.
(D) Xavier is eating pistachio.
(E) Xavier is eating rocky road.

23. If the two people who are sitting next to Yolanda are eating the same flavor of ice cream as each other, all of the following could be true EXCEPT:

(A) Ursula is eating orange sorbet and Victor is eating rocky road.
(B) Ursula is eating orange sorbet and Victor is eating strawberry.
(C) Ursula is eating rocky road and Victor is eating strawberry.
(D) Ursula is eating strawberry and Victor is eating orange sorbet.
(E) Ursula is eating strawberry and Victor is eating rocky road.

STOP
If you finish before time is up, you may check your work.
Solutions are on pages 124–125.

LOGIC GAME 1

A circus has six different acts during the first part of the show—balancing, diving, high wire, juggling, levitation, and trapeze—according to the following conditions:

- The second act is either juggling or levitation.
- The balancing act is immediately before the high wire act.
- If the diving act is first, then the juggling act is fourth.
- If the trapeze act is first, then the levitation act is fifth.

1. Which of the following could be a complete list of the six acts in the correct order?

   (A) balancing, juggling, high wire, levitation, trapeze, diving
   (B) diving, levitation, juggling, balancing, high wire, trapeze
   (C) diving, balancing, high wire, juggling, trapeze, levitation
   (D) trapeze, juggling, balancing, high wire, levitation, diving
   (E) trapeze, levitation, juggling, diving, balancing, high wire

2. If the trapeze act is fourth, which act must be fifth?

   (A) balancing
   (B) diving
   (C) high wire
   (D) juggling
   (E) levitation

3. If the diving act is fifth, which of the following is a complete list of the acts that could be third?

   (A) balancing
   (B) balancing, juggling
   (C) balancing, levitation
   (D) juggling, levitation
   (E) balancing, juggling, trapeze

4. If the trapeze act is sixth, which of the following statements must be FALSE?

(A) The juggling act is first.
(B) The juggling act is second.
(C) The levitation act is second.
(D) The balancing act is third.
(E) The diving act is fourth.

5. If the high wire act is sixth, which of the following is a complete list of the positions when the trapeze act could take place?

(A) third
(B) fourth
(C) first or third
(D) first or fourth
(E) third or fourth

6. The fourth act could be any of the following EXCEPT:

(A) balancing
(B) diving
(C) high wire
(D) levitation
(E) juggling

GO ON TO THE NEXT PAGE

LOGIC GAME 2

David is making a delivery of seven chicken dinners to three separate addresses on Lawson Street, Mulberry Street, and Newhall Street, though not necessarily in that order. Each dinner has a different number of pieces of chicken: 2, 3, 4, 5, 6, 8, or 10. At least one dinner is to be delivered to each house, according to the following parameters:

- The delivery to Lawson Street occurs sometime before the delivery to Mulberry Street.
- The delivery to Mulberry Street contains the 8-piece chicken dinner.
- The delivery to Newhall Street contains the 6-piece chicken dinner.
- The first delivery contains the 5-piece chicken dinner.
- The second delivery includes a total of exactly 12 pieces of chicken.

7.   If both the 2-piece and the 3-piece dinners go to the same house, which of the following statements must be true?

   (A) The 4-piece dinner goes to the house on Mulberry Street.
   (B) The 4-piece dinner goes to the house on Newhall Street.
   (C) The 10-piece dinner goes to the house on Lawson Street.
   (D) The 10-piece dinner goes to the house on Mulberry Street.
   (E) The 10-piece dinner goes to the house on Newhall Street.

8.   If the 10-piece dinner goes to the house on Mulberry Street, what is the maximum number of pieces of chicken that could go to the house on Lawson Street?

   (A) 3
   (B) 5
   (C) 6
   (D) 8
   (E) 12

9. If the delivery to Lawson Street includes exactly 15 pieces of chicken, which of the following statements must be true?

(A) The 2-piece dinner goes to Newhall Street.
(B) The 3-piece dinner goes to Mulberry Street.
(C) The 3-piece dinner goes to Newhall Street.
(D) The 4-piece dinner goes to Mulberry Street.
(E) The 4-piece dinner goes to Newhall Street.

10. If the third delivery includes both the 3-piece and the 4-piece dinners, how many pieces of chicken are in the order that is delivered to Newhall Street?

(A) 11
(B) 12
(C) 13
(D) 14
(E) 15

11. If exactly four of the seven dinners are delivered to Newhall Street, which of the following dinners must be included in this order?

(A) the 2-piece dinner
(B) the 3-piece dinner
(C) the 4-piece dinner
(D) the 5-piece dinner
(E) the 10-piece dinner

12. If the rule that the second delivery includes exactly 12 pieces of chicken is replaced by a rule that the second delivery includes exactly 14 pieces of chicken, what is the maximum number of pieces of chicken that could be included in the third delivery?

(A) 16 pieces
(B) 17 pieces
(C) 18 pieces
(D) 19 pieces
(E) 20 pieces

GO ON TO THE NEXT PAGE

LOGIC GAME 3

Eight debate team members—S, T, U, V, W, X, Y, and Z—participated in a competition, for which they were divided into two teams of four—the Green team and the Red team—according to the following conditions:

- If the Green team included T, then the Red team included V and X.
- If the Green team included U, then it also included T and Y.
- If the Red team included Z, then the Green team included S and V.

13. Which of the following could be a complete listing of the members who were on each team?

  (A) Green: S, T, U, Y
           Red: V, W, X, Z
  (B) Green: S, U, V, Y
           Red: T, W, X, Z
  (C) Green: S, V, W, X
           Red: T, U, Y, Z
  (D) Green: T, X, Y, Z
           Red: S, U, V, W
  (E) Green: V, W, X, Y
           Red: S, T, U, Z

14. If the Green team included U, which of the following must also have been on the Green team?

  (A) S
  (B) V
  (C) W
  (D) X
  (E) Z

15. If the Red team included T, which of the following must also have been on the Red team?

(A) U
(B) W
(C) X
(D) Y
(E) Z

16. Which of the following could NOT have been on the Green team along with W?

(A) S
(B) T
(C) U
(D) X
(E) Y

17. All of the following groups of four players could have been on the same team EXCEPT:

(A) S, U, Y, Z
(B) S, V, W, X
(C) T, W, Y, Z
(D) V, W, X, Z
(E) W, X, Y, Z

GO ON TO THE NEXT PAGE

LOGIC GAME 4

A theater featured films from eight different countries (Greece, Japan, Korea, Lithuania, Morocco, Norway, Poland, and Romania) on five consecutive nights. Each night, films from either one or two countries were shown.

- The second night featured films from Poland or Romania, or both.
- The third night featured films from Greece or Morocco, or both.
- The fourth night featured films from only one country.
- The films from Korea were shown one night before the films from Norway.
- The films from Japan were shown one night before the films from Lithuania.

18. Which of the following statements must be FALSE?

(A) The films from Korea were shown on the first day.
(B) The films from Japan were shown on the second day.
(C) The films from Romania were shown on the third day.
(D) The films from Poland were shown on the fourth day.
(E) The films from Lithuania were shown on the fifth day.

19. Films from each of the following pairs of countries could have been shown on the same day EXCEPT:

(A) Greece and Japan
(B) Japan and Romania
(C) Korea and Lithuania
(D) Korea and Poland
(E) Norway and Romania

20. If the films from Poland were shown on the third day, which of the following is a complete list of the countries from which films could have been shown on the second day?

(A) Japan, Korea, Romania
(B) Japan, Lithuania, Romania
(C) Korea, Norway, Romania
(D) Lithuania, Norway, Romania
(E) Japan, Korea, Lithuania, Norway, Romania

21. If the films from Korea had been shown on the second day, then which of the following statements CANNOT be true?

(A) The films from Greece were shown the day before the films from Japan.
(B) The films from Japan were shown the day before the films from Morocco.
(C) The films from Morocco were shown the day before the films from Japan.
(D) The films from Poland were shown the day before the films from Greece.
(E) The films from Romania were shown the day before the films from Lithuania.

22. If the films from Greece and Korea were both shown on the third day, which of the following statements CANNOT be true?

(A) The films from Japan and Morocco were shown on the same day.
(B) The films from Japan and Poland were shown on the same day.
(C) The films from Lithuania and Morocco were shown on the same day.
(D) The films from Lithuania and Poland were shown on the same day.
(E) The films from Morocco and Poland were shown on the same day.

23. Which of the following is a complete list of the days on which the films from Morocco could have been shown?

(A) 1st, 3rd, 5th
(B) 1st, 2nd, 3rd, 4th
(C) 1st, 2nd, 3rd, 5th
(D) 1st, 3rd, 4th, 5th
(E) 1st, 2nd, 3rd, 4th, 5th

STOP

If you finish before time is up, you may check your work.
Solutions are on pages 126–127.

ANSWERS

For each game, a shorthand version of all possible scenarios is provided before the answers, for reference. If an option is particularly unconstrained in one of the scenarios, it may be left blank.

Test 1

LOGIC GAME 1

1st	2nd	3rd	4th
HK	J	L	HK
HK	HK	J	L

1. (D) K, H, J, L
2. (D) K lives on the third floor.
3. (C) J does not live on the third floor.
4. (B) J does not live on the first floor.
5. (A) H lives on either the first floor or the fourth floor.

LOGIC GAME 2

Elected	Not elected
D, G	O, P, S
G, O	D, P, S
G, S	D, O, P
O, P	D, G, S

6. (E) elected: oncologist, psychiatrist
   not elected: dermatologist, gynecologist, surgeon
7. (B) the dermatologist and the oncologist
8. (E) dermatologist, oncologist, surgeon
9. (C) Either the dermatologist or the oncologist, but not both, was elected.
10. (E) Both the dermatologist and the surgeon were elected.
11. (B) Either the gynecologist or the oncologist, or both, must have been elected.

LOGIC GAME 3

Gemini	Libra	Scorpio	Taurus	Virgo
MN	MN	R	P	O
PR	M	PR	N	O
O	MN	R	P	MN
O	M	PR	N	PR

12. (B) Martina, Libra; Norah, Taurus; Oscar, Virgo; Philip, Gemini; Robert, Scorpio
13. (A) Martina's sign is Libra.
14. (B) Taurus
15. (D) Robert's sign is not Scorpio.
16. (D) Robert's sign is Scorpio.
17. (D) 3

LOGIC GAME 4

Top	Middle	Bottom
LP	S	V
L	PS	V
P	LV	S
P	L	SV

18. (B) top: football trophy, lava lamp
middle: photograph, stuffed animal
bottom: decorative box, vase
19. (C) The lava lamp is on the top shelf.
20. (D) the lava lamp and the vase
21. (E) The vase is on the bottom shelf.
22. (E) football trophy, photograph, vase
23. (A) The decorative box is on the middle shelf.

Test 2

LOGIC GAME 1

1st	2nd	3rd	4th
T	U	R or S	R or S
T	R or S	R or S	U
R or S	T	R or S	U

1. (D) Tyler, Samantha, Raymond, Ursula
2. (E) Tyler was interviewed second and Samantha was interviewed fourth.
3. (A) If Raymond was interviewed first, then Ursula was interviewed fourth.
4. (B) Raymond was interviewed immediately before Ursula.
5. (D) Samantha was interviewed fourth.

LOGIC GAME 2

North	East	South	West
H	G or I	F	G or I
H	F or G	I	F or G
G or I	H	G or I	F
F or G	H	F or G	I

6. (C) North: Gorman; East: Halliwell; South: Ivorsen; West: Forbes
7. (A) Gorman
8. (C) Gorman and Halliwell are partners.
9. (D) Ivorsen is not seated North.
10. (C) Gorman and Ivorsen are not partners.
11. (B) South

LOGIC GAME 3

Selected	Not selected
J, K, N	L, M, O
K, L, N	J, M, O
K, M, N	J, L, O
(JL), M, O	(JL), K, N

12. (E) N and O
13. (D) O
14. (E) If M and O are both selected, then L is also selected.
15. (E) none of the above
16. (C) N is selected but J is not selected.
17. (C) If K is selected, then O is not selected.

LOGIC GAME 4

Italy	Japan	Kenya
X	V, W	Y, Z
Y	V, W, Z	X
X, Y	Z	V, W
Y	X, Z	V, W

18. (B) Italy: Y; Japan: X and Z; Kenya: V and W
19. (C) V and W
20. (E) Y and Z
21. (C) Y is the only person who visits Italy.
22. (C) Aside from X, Z is the only other person who visits Japan.
23. (C) Kenya

Test 3

LOGIC GAME 1

Attend	*Do not attend*
Hong, Jarvis, Klein	Lofford, Nettis
Jarvis, Klein, Lofford	Hong, Nettis
Hong, Nettis	Jarvis, Klein, Lofford
Lofford, Nettis	Hong, Jarvis, Klein

1. (E) attend: Lofford, Nettis
        do not attend: Hong, Jarvis, Klein
2. (D) Jarvis and Nettis
3. (C) Jarvis and Klein
4. (A) Lofford
5. (B) Nettis attends the play and Jarvis does not.
6. (B) Exactly three people must attend the play.

LOGIC GAME 2

Grace or Maria	chicken
William or Zachary	peppers
Grace or William	sausage
Xavier	anchovies or olives
Grace, Maria, William, or Zachary	anchovies or olives

7. (E) Either William or Zachary orders the peppers.
8. (E) Zachary orders the anchovies.
9. (A) Maria orders the chicken but William doesn't order the
        peppers.
10. (D) 3
11. (D) 3

LOGIC GAME 3

1st	2nd	3rd	4th	5th
M or N	M or N	O or P	O or P	L
L	M or N	M or N	O	P
M or N	M or N	L	O or P	O or P

12. (D) Nora, Matt, Lana, Oliver, Paula
13. (C) Matt and Nora
14. (A) Lana stood directly in front of Nora.
15. (E) Nora and Paula
16. (D) Lana was fifth in line.
17. (E) Lana, Matt, Nora, Oliver, and Paula

LOGIC GAME 4

1: Q	2: R or V	1: V	2: Q or U
3: U	4: R or V	3: R	4: Q or U
5: S or T	6: S or T	5: S or T	6: S or T

18. (B) #1: Q #2: R
        #3: U #4: V
        #5: S #6: T
19. (E) U and V
20. (A) R and U
21. (A) Q and U
22. (E) T and U live on opposite sides of the street.
23. (B) R lives in either #3 or #4.

Test 4

LOGIC GAME 1

1st	2nd	3rd	4th	5th
S	P	B	F	T
S	T	B	P	F
P	S	F	B	T
T	S	P	B	F
P	T	S	F	B
T	P	S	F	B

1. (A) The man in the ten-gallon hat is first.
2. (D) The man in the ski cap is third.
3. (D) the men in the Panama hat and the ten-gallon hat
4. (C) The man wearing the ski cap is third.
5. (D) the men in the fedora and the ski cap
6. (B) The man wearing the ten-gallon hat is second.

LOGIC GAME 2

Hayes	Jackson	Lincoln
G, W	B, P	R, Y
G, W	P, Y	B, R
R, (GY)	P, W	B, (GY)

7. (B) Hayes: gold and white
   Jackson: purple and yellow
   Lincoln: black and red
8. (D) One of Jackson's colors is gold.
9. (A) One of Hayes's colors is gold.
10. (B) One of Jackson's colors is purple.
11. (B) One of Hayes's colors is gold and one of Lincoln's is red.
12. (B) Jackson
13. (B) yellow

LOGIC GAME 3

Selected	Not selected
D, E, F	G, H, J, K
D, F, H	E, G, J, K
D, J, K	E, F, G, H
F, G, H	D, E, J, K

14. (C) selected: D, J, and K
    not selected: E, F, G, and H
15. (B) D and J
16. (C) E and J
17. (D) F is selected and J is not selected.
18. (A) D and K

LOGIC GAME 4

1st	2nd	3rd	4th	5th	6th
R	N	R	N	R	N
N	N	R	N	R	N
R	N	R	N	N	R
N	N	R	N	N	R
R	N	N	R	N	R
N	R	N	R	N	R

19. (D) 2 or 3
20. (C) The second and fifth floors are both not rented.
21. (D) third and fifth
22. (B) the first and second floors
23. (A) if the second floor is rented

Test 5

LOGIC GAME 1

	2011		2012		2013	
	Spring	*Fall*	*Spring*	*Fall*	*Spring*	*Fall*
	LO	S	M			PR
	LO			S	M	PR

1. (C) Oslo, Lisbon, Rome, Stockholm, Madrid, Prague
2. (A) Lisbon
3. (A) Lisbon and Oslo
4. (D) Oslo, Madrid, Lisbon
5. (E) Lisbon, Oslo, and Stockholm
6. (A) Madrid and Oslo

LOGIC GAME 2

Cooks	*Doesn't cook*
K, T, V	I, J, S, W
I, K, (VW)	J, S, T, (VW)
J, S, (VW)	I, K, T, (VW)
K	I, S, T

7. (E) cooks: Jasmine, Scott, Wally
  doesn't cook: Iris, Kaylie, Tyrone, Victor
8. (B) Jasmine and Tyrone
9. (C) Kaylie cooks.
10. (E) Victor
11. (B) Jasmine and Scott both cook.
12. (A) Neither Scott nor Tyrone cooks.
13. (A) Iris cooks with two of her brothers.

LOGIC GAME 3

1	2	3	4	5
P	G	LPS		
P	L	P	G	S
P	L	S	GP	
S	G	LPS		
S	P	G	LP	
S	P	L	PS	G

14. (E) squats, push-ups, leg lifts, push-ups, glute crunches
15. (E) Her fifth set is glute crunches.
16. (C) Either her second or third set is glute crunches.
17. (E) Either her third or fifth set is leg lifts.
18. (C) Her third set is glute crunches.

LOGIC GAME 4

Scenario #1:		*Scenario #2:*	
UW	V	UW	UW
GI	GI	J	GI
UW	T	V	T
F	J	F	GI

19. (B) northwest: Wilton, Greek
northeast: Valencia, Italian
southwest: Ulrich, French
southeast: Thomsen, Japanese
20. (A) Ulrich's restaurant is north of Sunset Avenue.
21. (C) Valencia owns the French restaurant.
22. (C) Ulrich's Japanese restaurant is on the northwest corner.
23. (A) The French restaurant is on the southwest corner.

Test 6

LOGIC GAME 1

Soup	Entrée	Dessert
P	H	CD
T	HM	C
V	L	D
V	HM	BCD

1. (E) vegetable soup, meatloaf, chocolate cake
2. (E) chocolate cake, donut à la mode
3. (C) vegetable
4. (D) He orders the vegetable soup and the linguini.
5. (E) potato leek, tomato barley, vegetable

LOGIC GAME 2

1st	2nd	3nd
GM	RT	JPW
GM	PTW	JR
GPW	MT	JR
MPW	GR	JT
PW	GM	JRT

6. (B) first: Granger, Magyar
      second: Roseld, Taylor
      third: Jones, Perkins, Weld
7. (B) Perkins lives on the first floor.
8. (A) Granger and Magyar
9. (B) Magyar lives on the second floor.
10. (C) Jones, Taylor

LOGIC GAME 3

1st	2nd	3rd	4th	5th	6th
M	H	K	JPN	JPN	JN
N	H	K	M	P	J
N	H	K	P	M	J
M	J	H	K	P	N
M	J	N	P	H	K

11. (B) M, H, K, P, J, N
12. (D) M was ranked two positions higher than P.
13. (A) H, K, N
14. (C) K
15. (B) J was ranked sixth.
16. (B) N was ranked first and J was ranked second.
17. (B) second
18. (E) M and N had fewer than two employees ranked between them.

LOGIC GAME 4

Baseball	Football	Soccer
V, Y, (W, Z, ∅)	(V, ∅), Y, (W, Z, ∅)	(V, ∅), W, Y
V, (W, Z, ∅), (Y, ∅)	V, Y, (W, Z, ∅)	V, W, (Y, ∅)

19. (E) baseball: 3; football: 3; soccer: 2
20. (C) Vickery, Wade, Young
21. (E) Three of these students play on the football team and three
play on the soccer team.
22. (B) Vickery and Young
23. (D) Wade plays on both the football team and the soccer team.

Test 7

LOGIC GAME 1

Jul	Aug	Sep	Oct	Nov	Dec
K	L	F	G	M	H
K	L	F	H	M	G
F	L	M	H	K	G
M	L	F	H	K	G

1. (E) M, L, F, H, K, G
2. (D) L's birthday is in August.
3. (D) July, September, and November
4. (E) M was born in September.
5. (C) F, K, and M

LOGIC GAME 2

Selected		Not selected
F, K, V		A, B, T
F, V		A, B, K, T
K, (AF)	←B→	T, V, (AF)
T, (AF)	←B→	K, V, (AF)
B, (AF)		K, T, V, (AF)

6. (E) selected: Ford, Kia
        not selected: Audi, BMW, Toyota, Volvo
7. (E) the Volvo
8. (C) the Ford
9. (C) the Ford and the Kia
10. (B) Audi, BMW, Ford
11. (B) 3

LOGIC GAME 3

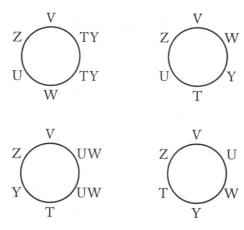

12. (C) Vasquez, Yeager, Taylor, Walker, Underwood, Zaines
13. (C) Walker and Yeager
14. (E) Walker and Zaines
15. (A) Taylor, Underwood, Vasquez
16. (A) Taylor
17. (B) Taylor and Zaines

LOGIC GAME 4

8:00	8:30	9:00	9:30	10:00	10:30
M	M	P	N	OQ	OQ
P	N	M	M	OQ	OQ
P	N	OQ	OQ	M	M

18. (E) P, N, O, Q, M
19. (D) M, O, P, Q
20. (A) N, O, Q
21. (B) 8:30 and 9:30
22. (D) P airs at 8:00 and M airs at 9:00.
23. (A) M airs immediately before P.

Test 8

LOGIC GAME 1

Mon	Tue	Wed	Thu	Fri	Sat
W	V	Y	U	Z	X
W	Y	V	U	Z	X
W	Y	U	V	Z	X
W	Y	U	Z	V	X
V	Y	U	Z	X	W
Y	V	U	Z	X	W
Y	U	V	Z	X	W
Y	U	Z	V	X	W

1. (C) W, Y, V, U, Z, X
2. (E) V, W, and Y
3. (E) Z
4. (A) Tuesday and Wednesday
5. (E) W checked in on Saturday.
6. (B) W

LOGIC GAME 2

Included		Not included	
K	RS	I	PT
IJ	S	KL	P
IJ	RT	KL	PS
IL	S	JK	
IL	T	JK	S

7. (E) Roger, Sven, Tomas
8. (B) Kate is included.
9. (E) Louisa is included and Tomas is not included.
10. (A) Jasmine and Pete
11. (C) Either Sven or Tomas is included, but not both of them.
12. (E) Kate and Pete

LOGIC GAME 3

1	2	3	4	5
MNp	S			
MNp		S		
MNp	Og	p	S	T
MNp	p	Og	Sp	T

13. (A) Ms. Minsky, Mr. Smith, Ms. Olsen, Mr. Truong, Ms. Norris
14. (B) She played Ms. Minsky the day before she played Mr. Smith.
15. (C) On the third day, she played pinochle with Mr. Smith.
16. (D) She played pinochle with Mr. Smith.
17. (D) She played Ms. Olsen two days before she played Mr. Truong.
18. (C) She played gin rummy with Ms. Norris and pinochle with Mr. Smith.

LOGIC GAME 4

(There are too many possible scenarios to show here; more information is required to narrow them down.)

19. (D) 6, 9, 12, 13, 19
20. (A) 5 (The game must have ended with 19, and the preceding cards, respectively, cannot be higher than 15, 11, 7, and 3.)
21. (B) 3
22. (C) 3, 4, 6 (We can eliminate 2, because 2 can never be the 2nd card played; only 1 can precede it, but 2 is not 3 greater than 1. The possible sets of plays are listed below.)

1st	2nd	3rd	4th
1	4	5	10
1	4	7	10
1	6	7	10
2	3	7	10
3	6	7	10

23. (D) 4 (the cards are 1, 2, 4, and 6)

Test 9

LOGIC GAME 1

Houston	Indianapolis
S, (TU), Y, Z	(TU), V, W, X
S, (TU), V, Z	(TU), W, X, Y
S, (TU), W, Y	(TU), V, X, Z
S, (TU), W, V	(TU), X, Y, Z
(SV), (TU), W, (XZ)	(SV), (TU), (XZ), Y

1. (E) Houston: U, V, W, Z
   Indianapolis: S, T, X, Y
2. (D) X and Z
3. (A) V and W
4. (E) Y
5. (D) T, V, W, X, Z
6. (D) X voted to hold the conference in Indianapolis.
7. (B) S, T, Y, and Z

LOGIC GAME 2

1:00	1:20	1:40	2:00
RT	(HJ)O	MW	(HJ)X
RT	(HJ)O	(HJ)X	MW
(HJ)T	(HJ)O	MW	RX
(HJ)T	(HJ)O	RX	MW
RT	HJ	OX	MW
RT	HJ	MW	OX
MW	HJ	TX	OR
MW	HJ	RT	OX

8. (D) Trevor entered at 1:40.
9. (C) Holly, Jenn, Olivia, Raoul
10. (A) 1:20
11. (D) Trevor entered at 1:00.
12. (C) Raoul

LOGIC GAME 3

1	2	3	4	5	6	7
M	F	HN	J	P	G	K
F	HM	J	N	G	P	K
G	M	F	HN	J	P	K
G	M	K	N	F	HP	J
F	H	JM	G	N	K	P
G	F	HM	J	N	K	P

13. (A) G
14. (D) N
15. (E) N
16. (D) 6th, 7th
17. (A) F
18. (E) J and P

LOGIC GAME 4

Fri eve.	Sat aft.	Sat eve.	Sun aft.	Sun eve.
W	RW	S		(QS)Y
W	SW	RW		(QS)Y

19. (E) Mr. Yeats has two evening performances.
20. (B) Ms. Quinn and Mr. Yeats
21. (A) Ms. Quinn appears on Friday evening and Mr. Yeats appears on Sunday afternoon.
22. (D) Mr. Yeats appears in exactly three performances.
23. (E) Mr. Yeats

Test 10

LOGIC GAME 1

1st	2nd	3rd	4th	5th	6th	7th	8th
W	Z	V	WZ	V	Z	V	W
W	V	Z	V	Z	W	VZ	W
W	V	Z	W	V	W	VZ	W
Z	W	V	WZ	V	Z	VW	Z
Z	VW	Z	V	Z	W	V	Z
Z	VW	Z	W	V	W	V	Z

1. (B) werewolves, vampires, zombies, vampires, zombies,
        werewolves, zombies, werewolves
2. (D) 3
3. (D) The fifth movie featured werewolves.
4. (D) 3
5. (E) sixth

LOGIC GAME 2

1st	2nd	3rd	4th	5th	6th
P	N	O	Q	S	R
P	O	S	Q	R	N
P	O	S	Q	N	R
P	O	S	N	Q	R
N	O	S	P	Q	R

6. (A) N, O, S, P, Q, R
7. (C) Q
8. (D) Q
9. (D) N, R, and S
10. (D) R
11. (C) Q

LOGIC GAME 3

1st	2nd	3rd	4th	5th
	s	Gv	F	Jp
Gv	s		F	p

12. (D) H, K, G, F, J
13. (D) She did a stencil for H.
14. (D) She did J's job third.
15. (B) F and J
16. (E) She did Palette Deco for K.
17. (B) F and G
18. (D) She did a stencil for either H or K.

LOGIC GAME 4

1st	2nd	3rd	4th	5th	6th	7th
H	-	R	P	-	-	T
T	-	H	P	R	-	-
R	P	H	-	T	-	-
-	T	-	H	P	R	-
-	R	P	H	-	T	-
-	-	T	-	H	P	R
-	-	R	P	H	-	T
T	-	-	P	R	-	H

19. (A) first
20. (C) second, fifth, sixth
21. (D) fifth, sixth
22. (C) On the fourth day she ran up a hill.
23. (C) up a hill, around a reservoir

Test 11

LOGIC GAME 1

Selected	Not selected
GHJK	I
GJK	HI
JK	GHI
GH	IK
G	HIK
I	GHJK
	GHIK

1. (B) Fran and Jessica
2. (C) Ivan
3. (E) Hank is selected.
4. (A) Hank is selected.
5. (E) Fran, Gloria, Ivan, Jessica

LOGIC GAME 2

1234	2345	3456	67		89
P	L	M	K	(JN)	G
	←—— FH,HF ——→				

6. (E) F, H, J, N, and P
7. (E) sixth
8. (C) L
9. (A) F and H
10. (D) N
11. (D) G, J, and N

LOGIC GAME 3

(There are too many possible scenarios to show here; more information is required to narrow them down.)

12. (C) blue, green, orange, blue, green, orange, red, blue
13. (C) blue, orange, red, yellow
14. (A) blue, green, yellow
15. (B) green
16. (D) green or orange
17. (C) orange
18. (C) 3

LOGIC GAME 4

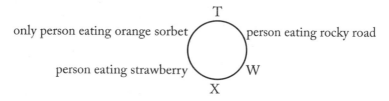

19. (D) pistachio, rocky road, strawberry
20. (C) orange sorbet, rocky road, strawberry
21. (B) rocky road
22. (D) Xavier is eating pistachio.
23. (A) Ursula is eating orange sorbet and Victor is eating rocky road.

Test 12

LOGIC GAME 1

1st	2nd	3rd	4th	5th	6th
T	J	B	H	L	D
D	L	T	J	B	H
JL	JL	B	H	DT	DT
JL	JL	DT	B	H	DT
JL	JL	DT	DT	B	H

1. (D) trapeze, juggling, balancing, high wire, levitation, diving
2. (A) balancing
3. (A) balancing
4. (E) The diving act is fourth.
5. (E) third or fourth
6. (D) levitation

LOGIC GAME 2

1st	2nd	3rd
L	M	N
5	4, 8 (and no others)	6
L	N	M
5	2, 4, 6 (and no others)	8
N	L	M
5, 6	2, 10 (and no others)	8

7. (A) The 4-piece dinner goes to the house on Mulberry Street.
8. (D) 8
9. (A) The 2-piece dinner goes to Newhall Street.
10. (A) 11
11. (B) the 3-piece dinner
12. (D) 19 pieces

LOGIC GAME 3

Green	Red
TUYZ	SVWX
TZ	UVX
Z	TU
SV	TUZ

13. (C) Green: S, V, W, X
        Red: T, U, Y, Z
14. (E) Z
15. (A) U
16. (C) U
17. (A) S, U, Y, Z

LOGIC GAME 4

1st	2nd	3rd	4th	5th
(JK)	(LN) & (PR)	(GM)	J or K only	(LN)
(JK)	(LN) & (PR)	(JK) & (GM)	L or N only	
	(JK) & (PR)	(LN) & (GM)	J or K only	(LN)

18. (D) The films from Poland were shown on the fourth day.
19. (C) Korea and Lithuania
20. (D) Lithuania, Norway, Romania
21. (E) The films from Romania were shown the day before the films
        from Lithuania.
22. (C) The films from Lithuania and Morocco were shown on the
        same day.
23. (A) 1st, 3rd, 5th

ABOUT THE AUTHOR

Mark Zegarelli is a writer, teacher, and puzzle creator. He solved his first logic puzzle when he was 8 years old and has been hooked ever since. In his teens, he started writing and publishing a weekly puzzle column in several local newspapers. Since then, he's published about 6,000 logic puzzles. He's also the author of eight "For Dummies" books on math and logic. His other books for Sterling include *Sit & Solve Boggle Logic Puzzles* and the upcoming *Mental Floss Extra-Strength Logic Puzzles*.

He is currently working on Simple Step Math, an online educational tool designed for the rapid acquisition and mastery of key math concepts and skills.

Mark splits his time between San Francisco, California, and Long Branch, New Jersey.